The Missing Course

WHY GRADUATES LIVE IN POVERTY
And How To Correct This In 33 Days!

ISBN:

Published in Nigeria by
RaphSoft Solutions
www.raphsofthost.com
info@raphsofthost.com
08186422209, 08052433258, 08051815725

Distributed by
Missing Course Books
info@
+2348052433258, +2348051815725

Contents

Acknowledgment

For every placement in life there is always a journey. And the journey of success is the roughest of all on earth. There are thorns and thistles on the road. There are seemingly insurmountable mountains and valleys to cross. No matter how rugged you are, you would always get a puncture or more. If you are not careful and carefree, you might be severely injured to the extent that after the wound has been healed, the scare will still remain. But this journey most times can be pleasurable, especially when you are journeying through the help of the Divine. There is nothing so motivating than to know that the Almighty God is always with you, even in the darkest moment. I give God all the glory for He has always been with me.

Irrespective of the level of unfaithfulness and lust in the world today, there are few persons that are embodiments of faithfulness and love. They are not acquaintances; they are friends. I believe that a friend is someone that comes in when others have gone out. Someone that has made up his or her mind to be with you, not minding your personality flaws. That is a friend! He or she corrects you when you are wrong and congratulates you when you are right. The person does not just tolerate you but celebrates you. Miss Abosede Shodeinde; you are a friend, a sister, a servant, a lover, God's instrument, and my World. Very soon you will reap all that you have sown.

I will not fail to appreciate my parents: My father, Mr. Edward Uyanwanne and my mother, Mrs. Theresa Uyanwanne. You will reap the fruits of your labour.

If I fail to appreciate your efforts in this book, then it's a great sin. Mr.& Mrs. Johnson Adejola, I know that you will also reap what you have sown. Rev & Pastor (Mrs.) N. C. Bernard, I know that you have contributed immensely to my life. May God reward you. I will not forget you; Kingston Nwosu for typesetting. I am really grateful to everybody that has contributed to my life and especially to this book. God will bless you all. You my reader, God will bless you abundantly; give you strength to receive all that is in this book and grace to be successful in everything you do. Happy reading!

Introduction
Don't Learn Too Late!
A man was about to die. So he called all his children and asked them to tell him how many times they would fail before they learn. One said three times, arguing that three is a perfect number. Another said two times. Another said just once. Then the youngest said to the father that he would not wait to fail before he would learn. That he would rather learn from the failures of others. And the father commended him for his wisdom. We have been made to believe that experience is the best teacher. However, I have seen many men and women who lived their lives in sorrows because of their yesterday's experiences. Others have become victims to the venom of poverty because of ignorance. Even after their lives have been revived the scars still remain. The difference between victims and victors is that victors learn before a problem occurs; victims learn after the problem has occurred. That is, victors learn before a trend, victims learn after the trend. One of the secrets of successful people is that they don't learn too late. Don't ever forget this!

"Many aspire but not all acquire." (E. A. Adeboye) But why is it not all that aspire that will acquire? Many expect but not all inspect. Why do many businesses flourish while others die? Why do many people succeed in life while others fail? Why do many people just try to survive when others are succeeding? Why do many educated people live in poverty while some uneducated ones are in wealth? Don't forget that wealth is fascinating; poverty is very frustrating. Don't you think so? Many people always give reasonable reasons why they failed. However, no reason is cogent enough to be a failure. And there is no mountain anywhere to cause your failure. Many people attribute their failures to the economy. If some are succeeding, then the economy is not just the problem. Many attribute their failure to their geographical location, educational background, sex or lack of enough start-up capital. Many young entrepreneurs always complain of lack of assistance. The question is this: Why do some entrepreneurs make remarkable business progress with just =N= 50,000, while others fail with more than =N=500,000 start-up capital? You don't need to travel abroad before you become a millionaire. It is possible in Nigeria.

I know that it's very frustrating for a young person to spend 4 to 6 years, or more, in the university or polytechnic only to graduate to become job seeker. Some are forced into being self-employed pending on when they are able to secure a 'better' job. Some could not tackle the obstacles that every self-employed person must face. So they quit too early, under the pretence that the economy of Nigeria is very bad. One thing is certain; there is no failure without a cause. The reason for this book is to show you ways you can overcome obstacles to life and wealth. Part one of this book will show you how education became the root of poverty in the world. Part two will reveal how we can overcome some key obstacles to financial success and fulfillment. Finally, in Part three we will explore the Money System.   If you follow everything wholeheartedly, you will one day shake hands with me in the city of wealth. I guarantee you this!

We are going to be curing the sickness and not the symptoms. Failure is a symptom of some problems. Getting more money to start that business again may not be what you need. If you don't solve the problem, you will definitely fail again. It is certain that mistakes are not bad, however, they delay progress. The intent of this exploration is for you to discover some of the things that will always cause failure in your life, which they don't teach in any school. Like I stated earlier, in Part two, I have carefully revealed some of the obstacles to success and the strategies used by great men and women to overcome them. You too can overcome them in just 33 days by conquering one problem every day. It is absolutely possible!

This book is written for everyone. Understand that wealth can bring happiness but how you acquire it will either bring joy or internal sadness. Celebration is not serenity. So if you want to make this money and have the peace and appetite to enjoy it, you must start applying certain principles into your life. And if you want to succeed in this world, you must be ready to do what those that have succeeded did. Learn how they overcame obstacles and you too will succeed. Also understand that you don't need to fail before you learn. You can learn from the failures of others.

I repeat my well-known slogan: If wealth were a product of schooling, then all professors would have become wealthy. People believe that if they go to school they would be wealthy. This is not correct. School was created to hide the secrete of wealth. That is why many educated people live in poverty. Why graduates live in poverty is because of some of the things they have been taught in the school. Reader, you will soon discover that most of the things you learn in school are responsible for most of your failures. Unbelievable! Isn't it? But that is the truth.

However, every failure is mostly caused by internal factors than external. Edmund Hillary once stated, "You do not conquer mountain but self." When things are not working, always look at the internal problems. If there is no internal obstacle, the external problems will have less effect on your life. This exploration will be aimed at eradicating or ameliorating the internal obstacles to success in life. As we explore these life-changing principles, allow them to change you, and people around you, then you will indeed change your life. You will never complete reading this book without experiencing remarkable changes in your life! Note this important weapon: Don't wait to be a victim before you learn. If you don't want to learn too late, then read on. Let's go!

Day 1
Stop Depending in Luck or Favour
I once heard a program coordinator said, "I prefer gifts to wages" According to him, it is better to receive a free gift than to work and receive your wage. There is nothing wrong about this; however, it is better to work your future than to live by gift, chance, luck or even

favour. Many people believe that whatever you achieve on earth is by luck. Some people call it grace, which they define as unmerited favor. But what is grace? And does it work for an idle person? If His grace is available for all, then why are some people poor and others wealthy? If grace means unmerited favour, why are we all not favoured? Many people keep wishing and waiting for favour; believing God that someday somebody will come to their rescue. David Oyedepo said, "God will do it is a slogan of an indolent." And I completely agree with him. The shortest route to failure is to depend on luck or favour. Nothing grows by chance. Every success in business and life is built on conscious efforts. Waiting for luck is allowing external forces to dictate for you. God cannot work for you without your cooperation. Better still, success in business and life generally, is not by nature but by nurture. Always understand that God is the source of every accomplishment but you are the instrument.

One of the principles I have learned from David Oyedepo is that you cannot get something from nothing. The miracle of sowing and reaping does not answer to affirmation. Success in life is not by favour but by labour. Not by luck but by work. You must do something that will bring favour. You must create your favour; you must work your luck. Favour is not free! David Oyedepo as a great pastor understands God's favour yet still believes in diligence. This book is not to showcase the success of any person, yet don't forget that this hero built the largest cathedral in the entire universe without any financial assistance from the western world or government. This is not luck or favour. It is a product of diligence.

Many people are trained 'receivers.' All through their school and after school lives, they have been trained to always receive from their parents. They prefer gift to income. They are always dependent. And this is a problem to wealth creation.

Don't forget the Law of Cause and Effects as deducted from the Aristotelian Law of Casualty. Don't also forget Isaac Newton Principle of motion, "For every action there is an equal and corresponding reaction." Ralph Waldo Emerson stated it this way, "Shallow men believe in luck; wise and strong men in cause and effects." What is the message? Every failure has a cause and every action has a result. You can overcome any obstacle by doing what great men did to overcome. The first obstacle all great people overcame is never to attribute success to luck or chance. Understand that anybody that is committed to applying some basic wealth producing principles will definitely become wealthy. Calvin Coolidge said, "Those who trust to chance must abide by the results of chance." Goethe said, "Woe to him who would ascribe something like reason to chance." Remember, it is not luck but work, not favour but labour that produces success. Will and Ariel Durant said, "Future never just happen, it was created." Alan Kay puts it this way, "The best way to predict the future is to invent it." Informed people understand that every future is created. But what does it take to create one? There are right tools for every innovation. Using the wrong tool will not only delay the work, but will increase the number of mistakes you will make, get you discouraged and make you a failure. This book is a 'Tool Box' for success in life. So read on!

Day 1 Exercise: Today, I want you to understand that gift is very good. Yet, you have to do everything possible to focus on work than luck. Change your belief, and understand that you can create your tomorrow. Don't just accept what you see; create what you want to see. The only way to do this is to stop receiving and start giving. Stop being dependent on your parents, spouse, friends, or any body. You will not die! The more you receive, the more relaxed you will become. And understand that until you are ready to die you may not live.

Day 2

Cultivating the Ability to Ask

Many people would do everything possible not to 'beg', because of their status, though they cannot differentiate begging from asking. And this is one of the reasons why they live in poverty. Every successful businessperson knows the importance of asking. Most millionaires are looking for where to invest their money. All they need is one new and productive idea. And they also know that they started their business journey by asking. But most graduates or young entrepreneurs never ask. They only complain or explain why their businesses are dwindling. In the book: How to Make Millions with Your Ideas, Dan S. Kennedy stated that one of the Millionaire-Maker Strategies is that if you don't ask, you will never get. You must ask. I do too. In school examination, asking is cheating. In life's examination, asking is cooperation. There was a time I went to my boss and asked, not for a raise in salary, anyway. I told him that increasing my salary would not solve my problem. I gave him some new business ideas and told him that if they bring profit we would share it. He agreed, even on a 50/50 basis. Both parties enjoyed the profits.

In my first book titled, "If You Want to be Wealthy, Don't be a Graduate", I told the story of Mark Andreessen. How he changed the Internet world with the Navigator web browser. What would have happened if Andreessen was waiting to get the money to develop the software himself? If he had not asked from Jim Clark, may be nobody would have heard about him. May be he would still be waiting. And may be another person would have come up with the same idea. The money you need to start that business is in the hands of somebody you know. You need to locate him and ask for it. If you keep waiting before you start, somebody else will start what is in your hand. I have told you not to be dependent on others, and I am telling you now to ask for assistance. Am I contradicting myself? No! Don't be a parasite and at the same time, you've got to ask. You have a dream. Sure! And you need help to accomplish it. But you have to ask for it. Get up and get to somebody. I know it's strange, because this is not what they taught you in school. However, don't undermine this! Just do it!

Day 2 Exercise: Simplicity can lead to negligence. Most principles are too simple that many people undermine them. Just like the principle of asking. It's so simple that people do not use it. Do not be tempted to undermine this principle because it's simple. I have discovered that there is no basic principle in life. If a principle did not produce the expected result, is because we have failed to apply it continuously for a long time. Stop complaining of your state. Stop explaining your situation to people. List the names of the people you know that have trust on you. And filter the names to the best ten. You are going to ask them for assistance. Don't beg! But you've got to ask. If you feel that this is not the right day to do this, then read Day 19, 24 and 29 of this book, before you do this exercise. You must know what to ask for, who to ask, where to ask and how to ask. Nobody wants to loose his or her money. So if you want to ask for financial assistance, then you must give the people assurance that their money is safe and that they must share in the profits. Also, don't accept a 'no' because a 'no' could later become a 'yes'. Now go!

Day 3

Overcoming the Fear of Making a Mistake

Many people are not advancing in life because they are afraid of the unknown. They don't want to make any mistake. Most graduates are so afraid of making mistakes. Mistake is an indication that you are doing something. Every mistake gives you an alternative route for advancement. It is better you attempt a thing and make a mistake than to be idle. Attempt is the unavoidable 'therapy' for every fear. So attempt it! Even if you make a mistake, attempt it again. Mistakes are not meant to stop you, but to teach you. Always remember that there is no great man today who did not make mistake yesterday. Action cures fear but indecision will fertilize it. Fear is the greatest virus to mankind. It kills abilities. It grows, it gathers momentum and it is transferable. The only way to overcome fear is to overcome the things you fear. Emerson once said that, "Do the things you fear and the death of fear is certain." To overcome fear in your life, tackle your confrontation with courage. Remember that it is better to die for a cause than to live for nothing. Robert Schuller stated, "Success is delivered to you most times on the platter of risk." And like Arch Bishop Idahosa once stated, "It is more risky not to take a risk." So be courageous and take the risk!

Educated people know the consequences of 'costly mistakes.' They make every necessary and unnecessary observation before they venture out. They are very calculative. They strongly believe in statistics. They understand price elasticity. They understand the Law of Demand and Supply. They are very careful. However, this is one of the reasons they live in poverty. Over the years, I have discovered that there are exceptions to every rule. It is called change. Read how Dale Carnegie puts It, "Take chance; all life is a chance. The man who gets farthest is generally the one who is willing to do and dare." The phrase 'take chance' means 'take risk.' Remember that those who take care never take charge. Look at men like Thomas Edison that tried about many times before he invented the candescent light. Don't stop trying because you 'failed.' One lesson from the life of Thomas Edison is that no matter how painful a mistake is, there is always a gain behind it. So don't waste the pain. Wake up and take the risk! Remember that quitters never win and winners never quit. So wake up!

Look at this wisdom by Nikki Giovanni; "Mistake are facts of life. It is the response to the error that counts." Don't pay more attention to caution else you will never advance in your life. Don't be too careful or careless, instead be carefree. On the other hand, never invest your fortune in any business you don't understand, because it may take you a great time to recover. Mistakes can delay progress.

Day 3 Exercise: Never invest your fortune in any business you don't understand, because it may take you a great time to recover. However, don't pay more attention to caution else you will never advance in your life. Don't be too careful. Don't be afraid of making that mistake. Sit down and think about some of the projects that you would have accomplished, but you are still waiting for the right time. The problem may be that you are afraid of making a mistake. Forget what the economy is like. Keep statistics out of this! Just do it! If you fail, do it again! You might need to run that business on part time first. Just like Mr. V said in Mafia Manager, "You do not test how deep a river is with both legs." Don't forget this!

Day 4

Overcoming the Fear of Criticism

Every criticism is an advice in disguise. So don't allow it to stop you. Every step in life attracts opposition and one form of opposition is criticism. Opposition comes to oppose your position. So you must oppose every opposition too, not by physical combat but by being doggedly committed to your business and life. Understand that everything whether good or bad must be criticized. Criticism is an indication that you are doing what others are not doing. Every plan will always look good until it is criticized. Criticism, most times shows the loopholes in your business plan. If somebody says that the strategy you want to implement is imperfect, sit down and device ways you can make it perfect. No matter how hard we try, there things we cannot make perfect. No criticism is destructive until you see it that way. Even if the aim of the critic is to stop you, he will never succeed without your cooperation.

When I published my first book, many graduates told me why it will not sale. That is it! They always see how things will not work. They told me that the title, 'If You Want to Be Wealthy, Don't Be a Graduate?' was not good. They also told me that it is an exclamation mark that should be used not a question mark. But the same book is now changing lives. We receive text messages and email almost every day from readers since the launching of the book. We also receive more calls every month, narrating the impact the book is making in the lives of people. Recently, I was opportune to be among some great pastors and a well respected pastor rubbished the book. He was so angry that he called me an anti-educationist. The same a week, a young man bought 30 copies of the book to share to people. According to him, "If this book could change my life to the extent of making me an employer of more than 13 persons, then I want it to change other lives also." I have people that are now CEOs of their companies because they read my book. Imagine if I had allowed criticism to stop me.

Another lesson I learnt from some great men is never waste your time defending yourself. Time will 'defend' you. I have seen men and women applying strategies they have criticized and rejected. No one imitates a failure. Understand that most people, especially your colleagues and those that believe that they know you very well, will never buy your ideas until they see results. Present your ideas but never waste time defending it. Most times we defend our idea we end up either magnifying it or modifying it. Also understand that if you wait to perfect everything before implementation, you may keep waiting till the end of the world.

Day 4 Exercise: Today what you will do is so funny. Just go to your spouse, friends, colleagues, pastor, parents or others and tell them about your new project. Surely, they will show you why the projects will not be accomplished. Whether they criticize it constructively or destructively, don't ever defend it. Don't allow them to stop you either, however, analyze everything critically. Somehow, they will show you what you were unable to see.
Day 5

Living above Past Failures

Many are handicapped today because of the failures of yesterday. You cannot succeed in life until you forget the failures of yesterday. The truth is that you have not failed until you give up. In the book,

The Magic of Thinking Big, David J Schwartz paraphrased one of the military slogans this way: "It is better to lose a battle and win the war than to win a battle and lose the war." War constitutes many battles. So what matters, is not how many battles you lose but who wins the war at last. Life is the war and every phase in life represents a battle. Forget the battles you have lost yesterday and strive to win the war at the end. Don't be crippled by your yesterday's failure for tomorrow holds something brighter for you.

One great skill that is lacking in our schools is the ability to manage failure, especially business failure. Most graduates do not understand anything about failures because they are not given opportunity to start or manage any business. The ability to manage failure is one of the most essential ingredients in wealth creation. From my personal experience I discovered that you could fail many times in life before you finally succeed. Most times you may lose your fortune. Understand what Zig Ziglar meant when he said that failure is an event not a person. You are not a failure; you only failed. I worked in a company where the CEO would always reject any new idea for advancement, on the ground that she once invested much into the company and it did not yield much. Her reply would always be; "Last two years I invested much into this business and my manager, Mr. XYZ mismanaged it." Today the company does not exist. Don't make this same mistake. In his book; Innovation and Entrepreneurship, Peter Drucker noted that one source of innovation is unexpected failure. So, use your today's pain for your tomorrows gain!

Think of the dream in the heart of Wernher Von Braun. The dream of exploring the moon, when everything about the topic was just mere fantasy. A dream he nurtured for about 35 years before it became a reality. Many of his experiments were not only failures but he was also put in jail in 1944. Later he was released from jail only to be forced to change his dream, from going to moon to building deadly rockets into space against England in the World War. Yet he persisted! The story of the first moon landing will never be told without a reference to his name.

As a history student in secondary school, I loved to read about the slave trade. One story I loved so well was the discovering of the New World in 1492 after the abolition of the slave trade. After Christopher Columbus had sailed to Africa, he began to think of how one could also sail to the west and find land. He asked the Portuguese Crown for support, they turned him down. He also tried the English leaders and they also did the same thing. He tried the Spanish government and they did worst. They turned him down after five years of delay. But Columbus persisted. And after many years his request was granted. He stayed about two months on the sea yet he did not give up. Even his sailors wanted to turn back, but he persisted. He discovered America.

What of Paul Galvin? He failed twice in business. I know what you would say, 'Is that all?' No, that is not all. He attended his own auction storage battery business. That is, he failed and the bank he owed decided to sell his company. And he was present at the meeting. With the last $750, he bought back the battery eliminator. If you have not read this story before, I want to state here that the battery eliminator later became what you know today as Motorola. Look at what he said at his retirement, "Do not fear mistake. You will know failure. Continue to reach out." Is your business down, and may be, your bank wants to sell it? Attend the auction meeting. And make sure you buy something from your own company. Who can tell, you could build another Motorola.

If Abraham Lincoln could still be the president after 30 years of failures, if Edmund Hillary could still climb the highest mountain after he lost one of his colleagues in the process, if Von Braun could still achieve his dream of going to the moon even when his dream was already killed, if Columbus could still discover America after the 'turn downs', if Edison could still invent the Candescent light after many times of failures, if Ford could still invent an automobile that majority of the people could afford after his sales men had discouraged him, if Paul Galvin could build a multinational company like Motorola from a battery eliminator, if Raphael could still own a company and publish a book after many years of hardship, then you too can succeed in life, irrespective of your circumstance. Just wake up and try again!

Day 5 Exercise: I want you to read this paragraph, 7 times and read it loud to yourself:

"If Abraham Lincoln could still be the president after 30 years of failures, if Edmund Hillary could still climb the highest mountain after he lost one of his colleagues in the process, if Von Braun could still achieve his dream of going to the moon even when his dream was already killed, if Columbus could still discover America after the 'turn downs', if Edison could still invent the Candescent light after many times of failures, if Ford could still invent an automobile that majority of the people could afford after his sales men had discouraged him, if Paul Galvin could build a multinational company like Motorola from a battery eliminator, if Raphael could still publish a book after many years of hardship, then I TOO CAN SUCCEED IN LIFE, IRRESPECTIVE OF MY CIRCUMSTANCE. Now, I will try this project again." (Mention the project in replacement of the word 'project.')

Day 6

Conquering Your Limitations

Many people are not successful in life because they believe that they are handicapped. A graduate of Computer Science once said to me, 'If only I could do my CCNA, I will have a good job with a good salary and live comfortably.' It is not bad do CCNA, but it's absolutely incorrect to depend on CCNA as the only platform for making more money. Most educated people are always limited people. However, nothing is a limitation! It sounds strange but that is the truth.

Sickness is not a handicap, physical deformities are no handicap, and illiteracy is not a handicap. The only handicap that exists is 'mental handicap' or what can be termed 'sense deficiency.' That is, lacking what to do to advance in your life. If people like Henry Ford,

Thomas Edison and others could succeed in life without adequate formal education. Don't forget that Bill Gates, one of the richest men on earth was not a graduate before embarking on his business journey. Don't ever allow your state to determine your status. I have come to know that the problem you face in your business may bring a new business idea to you. For example, if you produce fruit juice and you have problem getting the raw materials. If you can solve this problem, you may end up supplying raw materials to other companies that have similar problems. As the business grows, you may be manufacturing the raw materials.

One lesson from the life of Bill Gates is that what is available to you is enough for a start, if you have enough ideas. I have come across great men who became great because they saw their inabilities as assets. I once saw an artist, paralyzed in both hands and legs, yet draws with his mouth and made beautiful artistic frames he sales. I saw a pastor, blind yet pastor's a great congregation. Another pastor lost his two feet, yet had many pastors working under him. I once met a man that just recovered from leprosy, no toes, yet he is one of the best comedians I have ever met, bringing joy to many people and putting money in his pocket.

Look at people like Lionel Barrymore. He made full proof of his abilities on wheelchair. What of Fanny Crosby, blind yet became a pianist, harpist and composed about 8,000 songs. I read about Putty Wilson, an epileptic, yet noted to have run 1,300 miles race. She became what she wanted to be. Helen Keller was blind, deaf and dumb yet wrote 27 books. What of the one time president of America Franklin D Roosevelt, who became president on wheelchair?

Many successful people never had good educational background or never even went to school. I want to repeat my slogan here again, as I repeated it many times in my first book on Missing Course series titled, If You Want To Be Wealthy, Don't Be A Graduate? I maintained that if wealth were a product of schooling, then all professors would have become wealthy. But this is not so. Williams Shakespeare was only a modern school graduate. Somebody said, "I am not succeeding in my business because I am not intelligent." No one is intelligent, what we have are diligent people. It is diligence that makes you intelligent. I once said to some students that you do not pass your exams because you are intelligent but you pass because of your diligence. Every business guru is a product of diligence, because diligence will always make a success out of a failure. Many people believe that they would have become wealthy if they had gone to the university. However, some graduates still believe that the reason they are living in poverty is because they don't have enough start-up capital and no body to help them. That is it! Everyone with an excuse. The truth is this: If you have this same belief, you will hardly ever become wealthy. You have to conquer that limitation from your mind.

Geographical location is also not a limitation. If you live in Nigeria, for example, whether you live in a remote place in Kano State or in Victoria Island in Lagos State is irrelevant. There is no location in this world that God's allocation cannot reach. What will make you is not where you live but what lives in you. Whether you live in New York City in America or Dar El Salaam, Tanzania is irrelevant. Whether America or Switzerland has the highest capital income in the world, and you are not from these two countries is not a limitation. You don't need to come to Ikeja in Lagos State, before you can start a computer business. That is true!

Day 6 Exercise: By now you are expected to have forgotten your failures of yesterday. But today what you will do is to take a pen and write down the stories of your failures. Then ponder on each story. Why did you fail? Did you later overcome? How? List one lesson you learned from each failure. Out of all the projects you failed to accomplish, which one is still burning in your heart? What do you have right now to start with? Get up right now and start! (Note: Before you start that project again, you may need to go through Day 18, 22 and 27.)

Day 7

Breaking the Shell of Your Past Success

Myles Munroe once stated in a leadership summit that, "The greatest enemy to your future is your last success." Both past failure and past success can cripple ones life. Many people over celebrate their past success to the extent that they became contented with where they are. If where you are is not your final address then you are still on a journey. The point is that success is a journey. There is nothing that drains abilities than I-have-arrived-mentality. For the fact that you implemented an idea yesterday, and you had a boom does not mean that the same idea will also produce the same result tomorrow. In the world of success imitation has always been the greatest problem. Others will always do what you did, and perhaps get the result you got, or even better. If you have to remain on top, never depend on your last success. One of the problems in life is to believe that you can be doing the same thing and get a better result. I always say that there is no advancement in life without an adjustment. Ponder on that!

Most educated people are proud people. Forgive me, but that is the truth. To spend 4 to 6 years in the university is indeed a great success to them. I also think that it's not too easy too. Anyway, that does not make you better in the real world. We have considered Henry Ford as a success, and indeed he is. But why did Ford lost market shares to competitors like General Motors? He failed to understand that the fastest thing on earth is change. He refused to upgrade or replace his model-T car on time, irrespective of the ideas from his subordinates, because he was at the peak of business success. One lesson: Never sit down on the seat of success.

John D. Rockefeller was the richest man in the world in his time. A successful businessman, and the brain behind Standard Oil Company. However, he 'sat down on the seat of success.' He made his money through kerosene and did not believe in gasoline because the future of automobile at that time was bleak. He even terminated the appointment of one of his managers because the manager wanted to focus on gasoline production. Today, gasoline has changed the entire world.

Certificate is not a measure of success. Always change with every change. Another lesson from the millionaires is this: "Never think like a successful person or you will soon fail." I borrowed that statement from Bill Gates, Okay! In conclusion, I want you to understand that your certificate just adds to your status. Certificate is not a treasure. One of the greatest treasures in the real world is knowledge. Wake up!

Day 7 Exercise: Today you are going to evaluate yourself. Know where you are. Ask yourself some relevant questions. Where you are today, is that where you should be? Why are you still there? Is it because you thought that you have arrived? And how long have you been there? Are you really doing anything to leave there? Do you see your certificate as a success or as a means to success?

Day 8

Living Above Riches

Many people measure success by the amount of riches they have accumulated, which is not correct. Quick riches can minimize your abilities and leave you unfulfilled. I like this statement by Charles Kingsley, he said, "We act as though comfort and luxury were the chief requirements in life, when all that we need to make us really happy is something to be enthusiastic about" One thing about quick riches is that they can disappear the same way they appeared. Your money is not useful until it can work for you. It is one thing to have money; it is another thing to use the money productively. You don't spend money; you don't keep money; you invest money. Make your money work for you!

Most educated people have one thing in common; they always equate financial security with financial freedom. Informed people know the difference. One thing I learnt from Rich Dad's Prophecy is that security is not freedom. The more secured you are the less freedom you have. In the business world there is no financial security, but there is financial freedom. The difference is simply control. If you have control over your cash flow, you will soon have financial freedom. One day I saw some group of people that are waiting for their retirement funds - we call them pensioners. Educated but uninformed people. They were really ridiculed by abject poverty. They were seriously complaining on the television about the government's insensitivity to their demands. May be they were right; however, their problem was not the government but lack of control over their life. I wish they had discovered, even if it is a little late, that they should have control over their income. Remember that many of them were rich when they were in service. They assumed they were secured, not knowing that there is nothing called financial security in the world of success. This is a great lesson every graduate, employee or new entrepreneur must learn. You are not secured until you have total control over your cash flow.

Another thing is this: To be wealthy is not to be rich. Read my first book titled, If You Want To Wealthy, Don't Be A Graduate? You will know the difference between riches and wealth. I will keep making reference to this book. Remember that this book you are reading is a sequel to it. The point is this: You are not successful because you are rich; you are successful when you become wealthy. The next paragraph will explain this.

I read an article sometimes ago that shocked me. This was about a great musician MC Hammer. The article was titled, 'Hammer Falls On MC.' According to Forbes Magazine, MC Hammer was once listed in the world richest entertainers with income of $33 Million. After just 5 years (from 1991 to 1996) more than 300 creditors were queuing for a share of Hammer's remaining assets. He was indebted to the sum of $14 million. What was the problem? He was only rich; he was not wealthy. MC Hammer made his money too quick. As a musician, he became a rap star and rich when his rap song "U Can't touch This" became the best rap song in history. Because he did not understand the difference between riches and wealth he began to buy liabilities instead of assets. He acquired 17 cars, including a 1975 Mercedes, a 1990 Ferrari and a limousine that is so long that it carried 13 people. At a time his entourage were about 47 people, including dancers, singers, security men, personal disc jockeys, musicians, etc. which he flew around in his own Boeing 727. He was busy consuming not investing. He had a mansion in 12 acres of land. The stereo in his bedroom cost $300,000. There is a waterfall right inside the house. He had a wall of television screen that enabled him to watch 27 channels at once. The lavatory in his house was with a gold-plated seat. But a time came when Hammer began to beg for loan, could no longer pay his tax and now put his mansion for sale at $5.6 million, which could not even pay his debts. From $33 million income a year to $14 million debt. You can see that one can be rich today and poor tomorrow. I know that you will not allow this to happen to you!

Day 8 Exercise: Your duty today is to read chapter 5 of my book, titled, "If You Want To Be Wealthy, Don't Be A Graduate?" The chapter's title is The Missing Course. Even if you have read it before, you need to read it again.

Day 9
Trading Pleasure for Pressure
Pleasure can never instigate you for action. Discipline yourself, because there is no attainment in life outside discipline. Check those that are very good in merriment, they can never be wealthy in life. A good businessperson mustn't eat any part of his or her capital. Business establishment is not business success. That you established a business is not a guarantee for success. You do not spend money until you have succeeded. It is better to starve today and eat tomorrow. Let it not be the other way round. Every one must be able to differentiate his wants from his needs. Get what you need but never satisfy your wants until you have succeeded. Never take a loan on what you will wear or eat. Don't eat the loan you take; invest it. I know a businessman that would take a loan with the intention of investing it; however, he would always use part of the loan for self-gratification. The result is that he has never been able to pay all his debt. One of the laws of success is that you must delay every immediate gratification for future benefits. I think that it is better to suffer the pressure of today in order to have the pleasures of tomorrow. Don't you think so?

Many graduates have never in their lives multiplied money. Some can manage what they have, but they have never tried to multiply it. And it is the process of multiplying money that you will know if you can overcome pressure or not. Educated people are trained spenders. It is very few that can invest. Even when the few want to invest, they always want to start from the top to meet their status. Reader, if you want to fail then start from the top.

Don't rent a shop for a telephone service business when all you have as start-up capital is below =N= 50,000. You can use a kiosk. Most educated people will employ a secretary, a receptionist, a personal assistant, a timekeeper, when all they have as start-up capital is below a million naira. Understand that you may need to pay salary from your start-up capital for 2 to 3 months. Not every business will produce profits immediately it is established. Business success is in stages, and failure to understand the stage you are may cause failure. Don't forget that Brain Tracy, author of some the bestseller business books, started his business carrier in his car. He was even living in his car. Publius Syrus said, "If you wish to reach the highest, begin at the lowest." The shortest route to the top is through the bottom. Read this last statement again.

Day 9 Exercise: Have you ever multiplied money? No. Then you need to start today, even if everything is okay with you financially. This is one lesson you will never learn from the University. If you have generated or multiplied money before or you are still doing it but need to do more, then what you need is to differentiate what you need from what you want. Necessity is different from desire. Start accomplishing the necessary things and undermine your desires. Your desires will be fulfilled when all necessities are accomplished. So you are to use today to different your needs from you wants. Then focus on accomplishing your needs.

Day 10

Understanding Success

I have always defined success in all my seminars and writings. So I am going to do just that here, because you must understand what you want to become. Success is not status or title, not a position, not your accumulation, not your collection, not your derivation. Success is simply defined by the quality of your services.

During the question and answer section in a seminar, a young man stated, after he had listened to my speech on 'If You Want To Be Wealthy, Don't Be A Graduate?' He said: "You defined success as ones contribution and not his or her position. Professors contribute more to the world. If this is the measure of success, then professors are the most successful people. Yet throughout your speech you keep stating that 'If success were a product of education, then all professors would have become successful.' How do you reconcile this?"

Now, I am going to give you the same illustration I gave my audience in that seminar: Sure, professors are very active people. A visit to their offices will confirm this. However, one of the problems I saw in the school is that professors are very active, yet many have nothing to show for their activities. Successful professors are those that understand the difference between being active and being productive. There is a big difference between effectiveness and efficiency. When you are active, your employer pays you. But when you are productive, you get paid both by your employer and your result. Most times, the world keeps paying you, even after your death. Professors contribute to the world, however, the world reward only those that contribute productively not actively. The world will keep paying you if you can serve them productively. I want you to take note of this: If you can give to the world what they need most or take away from them what they hate most, then you will become successful beyond measure. It is called services!

You have not succeeded until you have been able to build for yourself, chains of customers that are committed to you because of the services they get from you. You have not succeeded in business until your business grows to the level where your absence does not reduce the profits you make. Answer this question: How will your business be if you die? Will the business die with you? Success without a successor is absolute failure. Think about that!

Educated people believe that success is your status or your position. Success is not status but service. It is not surplus but sacrifice. It is not your position but your disposition. It is not your collection but your contribution. It is not what you derive but what you donate. Your level success is defined by your integrity not your dignity. If you cannot sustain your level of success, you have not succeeded. And integrity sustains success. Integrity means to be consistent. A man with utmost integrity knows that all clients are important, and that no one is more important than another. Thomas Carlyle puts it this way, "You can tell a big person by the way he treats little people." Failure to understand this will definitely lead to failure in life no matter how successful you are today. The two basic ways to sustain success is to meet people's needs or their wants. Remember, needs are necessities; wants are desires. If you can keep meeting their necessities or keep providing them with their desires, you will never fail in life. In the book; The 100 absolute unbreakable laws of business success by Brian Tracy, he stated that, "Customers are both demanding and ruthless; they reward highly those companies that serve them best and allow those companies that serve them poorly to fail." Yes! Customers reward integrity and service.

Most companies started with integrity, and it indeed built their dignity. As the company grows, some have traded integrity for dignity. At this level some companies begin to reward proficiency and undermine potential. Some even consider competence more than character. They begin to hire those that will work for them and not those that will work with them. There are two types of employee: Those that are working for you and those that are working with you. The difference is not competence but character. I always say that any employee that is overwhelmingly aware of the need to get customers and keep the existing ones is not just working for you but working with you. Let's look at the difference:

Anyone that is working for you is working to live. Anyone that is working with you is living to work. Anyone that scales through during the aptitude test will definitely work for you, if your terms are acceptable by him or her. Some of these employees are working just to earn a living, which is detrimental to any organization. They are simply working for money. (Note: Don't ever work just to earn. It is better in the long run to work to learn.) On the other hand, few employees are working for their future. They undermine every immediate profit for a more viable reward. That is attitude not aptitude. One of the reasons graduates live in poverty is because they have been trained to work to earn instead of to work to learn. Every person must not forget this simple but fruitful key. I will explain more about this later.

Don't also forget that success is character. Success is positive attitude. Failure is always knocking at the doors of success. Don't open the doors by undermining these truths! You are warned.

Day 10 Exercise: Change your understanding about success. Understand that success is about service not surplus. Remember that if you can give to the world what they need most or take away from them what they hate most, then you will become successful beyond measure. Now think very well. What do think you can do that will make the world to keep paying even after your death? Write it down and begin to work on it.

Day 11
Breaking the Traditions
Many educated people are where they are today because they have identified themselves with the Status Quo of our society. I observed that Status Quo is a Latin word for "The mess we're in." No man that has accepted the usual way of doing things can ever succeed in life. When you assume or conclude that something cannot be done in a new way, you limit your abilities. You limit the amount of effort you make. And productivity is measured by the amount of effort displayed. Success demands that you do the unusual and the extraordinary. Many good authors have written on the laws of success, however, I have also discovered that there are laws that must be contravened before you can succeed in life. For example, there is a business law that states that you should not put all your eggs in one basket. Meaning that, you should diversify. However, diversity in business is not spreading your fortune into many different businesses. Diversity is doing one business in different ways. Using many strategies to do one business is diversity. That is

putting all your eggs into one basket then focusing on that one basket with every strategy you know.

We go school to learn the traditions. That is why educated people believe in keeping the rules and regulations of their professions. And that is why many live in poverty. In this world, you may need to invent an entirely new rule or amend an existing one before you can succeed. John Mason said, "Yesterday's formula for success is often tomorrow's recipe for failure." Remember what Thomas Watson, the founder of IBM said, "There is a world market for about 5 computers." I wonder what IBM would have become if he hadn't changed their product immediately the market changed. We are going to examine the life of Mr. Watson later in this book. One basic advantage of this age is that any entrepreneur can take on multinational companies and win. Today, there is a great change in business world, though many entrepreneurs in this part of the world still undermine this change. Anyone that takes advantage of this change will definitely become a millionaire in a short time. It is not effectiveness that counts now, but efficiency. We are in the era of speed and accuracy. The great change is the Internet!

Educated people understand that there is no success without service. And many of them serve but have nothing to show for their services. We are in the era where effectiveness has given way for efficiency. The world reward efficiency, but only award effectiveness. Award is a compliment; reward is compensation. In the world of success, how efficient you are will determine how productive you will be. Effectiveness is measured by your effort; efficiency is about results. Success is about your result not your effort. But what is the difference between effectiveness and efficiency?

Assuming you are a businessman, and you are having many customers all over the country. You want to announce to them about your new products. If you decide to post the letters through the post office or take the letters to their houses personally, you are only being active. If you decide to use the service of a courier, and may be they were able to get the mail in three days, then you are effective. If you are smart enough to get the email addresses of all your customers through your website, using an AutoResponder or a mailing list, then you are efficient. Now you understand the difference.

It is not about working harder; it is about working smarter. Efficiency is about the speed, cost and accuracy of your result. How fast were you able to produce the result? What is the cost of the result in relation to the benefits of it? And how accurate is the result? Remember that in this era, it is not brute power that produces result but brainpower. And how efficient you are is dependable on your mental prowess.

Many entrepreneurs still use the old approach the snail mail to mail their customers. They spend more money. And what of the slow process of transaction? With a Mailing List you can reach all your customers in 5 minutes or less. With a Website and an AutoResponder you can capture any prospective customers and keep him or her for life. We are in the age where you don't need to leave the comfort of your home to purchase a product. You can transact a business via the Internet, and get your goods or services without leaving the comfort of your home. Warning: If you are a businessperson, whether new or old, you need a website. It is not as expensive as you think. You can even register for free hosting. You don't have to pay for registration or hosting and you can build it yourself. If you need more information on this, send a mail with subject: Free Website, to uyanwanneraphael@yahoo.com. Better still, with =N= 20,000 or less you can have a complete website with personal email addresses, Mailing Lists, AutoReponder, easy to use Control Panel, etc.

Day 11 Exercise: There are two things you will do today. One: Contravene! Think of a way of changing the normal method of executing that project. How can you change that well-known tradition of carrying out your business? Two: Own a website for your business. Begin the preparation today. If you want to know more then send me an email.

Day 12

Disassociate with Wrong Associations

"The future of every seed is in the soil," says a wise man. The future of every person is highly dependable on the company he keeps. Every company or relationship that de-motivates you limits your abilities. And motivation is a compulsory element in life. The fastest way to grow in life and business is through networking. Every person is dependent on another. Failure to appreciate this fact may retard your growth. No independent person will ever succeed. You need people to succeed in life. However, getting the wrong people is the shortest route to bankruptcy. The educated believes that you cannot make 100 percent of spare parts dealers your companion when you sell jewelry. That is correct! That is why lawyers associate with lawyers, doctors relate with doctors, engineers network with their fellow engineers, etc. However, I want you to read this loud: It is better for a doctor to relate with a lawyer with a positive mental attitude than to relate with a fellow doctor with a negative mental attitude.

Warren Buffet was once the richest man in America before he later relinquished this title to Bill Gates. Irrespective of the age gap, these two entrepreneurs are close friends. Why? Why was Zig Ziglar a friend to Norman Vincent Pearl? Why is John Maxwell a friend to Myles Munroe? Why are Brain Tracy, Jim Rohn, Les Brown, Zig Ziglar friends? Why is Ayo Arowolo a friend to Sunny Obazu-Ojeagbase? Why is David Oyedepo a friend to Myles Munroe, Mike Murdock and Matthew Ashimolowo? You may say that they are in the same profession. But I will say because they are people with positive mental attitude. Who are your friends? Your companions should be people that share the same interest with you. People that are positive are better than people in your profession. Please don't play with this! If you want to make it, then disassociate with wrong associations.

Day 12 Exercise: Your association can correct you or corrupt you. So today you have to write down all the names the people you associate with. Evaluate the impact each person has made in your life, whether negative or positive. Then disassociate with those with negative impact. Please don't play with this. You are warned!

Day 13
Overcoming Imaginary Difficulties

Difficulties are bound to come as you embark on this journey. As I always say; 'There is no advancement without adversity, no pleasure without pressure, no breakthrough without passing through.' Yet don't allow imaginary difficulties to stop you from trying a thing. I always say to people that I don't have any problem; all I have are challenges, which are channels for my manifestation. So don't use your mind to create problems, for there is nothing called problem outside your imagination. Remember that only you can defeat yourself. One of the weapons I have always used in solving problems is to understand that every problem has an expiring date. And that I, most times, determine the expiring date. I have also come to know that most of the problems we envisage in our businesses or life never materialize. An educated man came to me with what he called a business plan. All I read in the business plan were obstacle to his future business - ways his proposed business will not work - and no written plan on how to overcome the obstacles. That is imaginary difficulties not a business plan. If you took reasonable time to write your business obstacles, also take double of that time to write the overcoming principles. Understand that any obstacle you predict is a question you must answer. And you can, if you do.

A Graduate collected a magazine that is published here in Nigeria from me. And after going through it, he said, 'I have studied this very well. The problem is that it will not work here in Nigeria because I have also taken time to study our economy.' Now, what was the problem? Because of his profession as an economist, his mind created many reasons why it will not work, and this is based on the courses he had learned in the school. Today people are making millions of Naira from Cassava flour. That was the business that would not work in Nigeria. My graduate friend is still living in poverty.

Jim Reeves, one of the old country music artists, said, "Every road has a bending." John Mason puts it this way; "You can't travel the road to success without a puncture or two." In conclusion, he writes,

"The man who invented the eraser had the human race pretty well sized up. You will find that people who never make mistakes never make anything else." Louis Boone said, "Don't fear failure so much that you refuse to try new things. The saddest summary of life contains three descriptions, could have, might have, and should have." The most dreadful thing on earth is to end your journey with 'had I known.' Think of that project that you have failed to start because of the obstacle you foresee. In every adversity is an advantage for advancement. While you ponder on that last statement, I want to show you the weapons I have used many times to overcome obstacles. I discovered them from the lives of some millionaires. I have shared them in meetings and in some of my articles. And they always produce remarkable results. So use them!

1.   Patience, persistence and perseverance.
        This is called the principle of the 3Ps. I am going to write more on this in one of the proceeding chapters.
2.   Don't share your problem with people that would not solve it
        Is there any difficulty you foresee? Mark those you share it with. No matter what the person is to you, if he or she cannot contribute to the solution, then don't share it with him or her.
3.   Know that no problem will last forever
        Like I have always stated every problem has an expiring date. Even if you've lost all and you're contemplating starting again. Just read this, "Look at what you have left, never look at what   you have lost." (Robert Schuller.) "Between you and anything   significant will be giants in your path." (Bob Harrison.) Let me ask you this question: Is your circumstance an instrument or a disease? Hold your answer!
4.   Be ready to do something that you did not plan for.
        There is a funny adage in my language that states that, "When a tailor makes a mistake, it automatically becomes a style." As a graphical artist, I have discovered that most designs are never conceived beforehand. They come as you place the right hand on the mouse and the left hand on the keyboard. You never planned them! This is the summary of life. So start the business, because the error that counts may produce the profits that matter. All you need to do is to adjust when necessary. And let's look at that:

5.   **Always be ready to make a change**
There is no advancement without adjustment. Like John Patternson commented, "Only fools and dead men don't change their minds. Fools won't change. Dead men can't" Change is one of the things you cannot run away from else you become unhappy all the days of you life. I know you need results. But it can't come until there is a change. Don't change your business; change your strategies. Don't change the principle either; change the procedures. Change your techniques, your methods, your tactics. It counts!

6.   **Take time to solve your problems**
Every true millionaire will agree with me that it takes time to solve a problem. Is there a problem in your business? Then give it time. Not just time but adequate time. Don't rush! Action is the keyword in business; yet don't be too fast for your   God.

7.   **If you cannot solve your problem then manage it**
I took this principle from Napoleon Hill, Norman Vincent Pearl and Robert Schuller books. There are problems you have to manage until they are completely solved. No matter how hard you try, you may not be able to solve them, except there is a supernatural intervention such as miracle or magic. For example, you want to start a catering business but you are   physically blind. What do you do about that? Consider this example: One of my cousins served a man for some years with an unwritten agreement that the man would establish a business for him at the end of the service. Some months before the end of the service, the man said that some money was missing. He then concluded that my cousin stole the money. He decided not to establish the business for him. We had to look for an alternative. Why? Time will surely heal the wound. You've got to move on! Just keep on keeping on!

8.   **In times of problem, remember your last victory**
Every man had in time past solved a problem. No matter the enormity and peculiarity of your problem, if you've not solved such problem before, somebody somewhere somehow has solved the same problem. So you too can! All you need

to do is to remember your last victory. The problems we shy away from today are the giants of tomorrow. I believe that this is one of the secrets of King David in the Bible. While goliath was busy abusing him, he was also busy reciting his victories - how he defeated Lion and Bear and he became victorious again.

9. Then restrict your problem to yourself and God

There is joy and confidence that springs from somewhere when you know that there is a higher Being with you. Why do people say, "I just feel like sharing this with someone?" If you believe that sharing a problem with a friend can ameliorate it, then God is more than a friend. Irrespective of your religion, you've got to pray, if not all the times but sometimes, especially when you are in a problem.

10. Now begin to see the good side of your problem

Your perception of problems ultimately determines its fruits. Whether you will have a hopeless end or an endless hope lies in your ability to manage any problem that comes your way. I want you to understand that the seed of today are the fruits of tomorrow. Every action you take is a seed that will guarantee a harvest. If you cannot see the good side of your problems, you will always take wrong actions. You will always react instead of responding. You will always complain and explain, and none of these ever produces positive result.

11. Be joyful

Always love what you have. Value it. Cherish it. Don't complain of what you don't have but rejoice over what you have. When you love what you have, you will be excited. And excitement brings motivation and motivation is the number one force of fulfillment in life. No matter what you have and where you are, always appreciate yourself. For little is much when God is in it. No success is automatic. For every position in life there is always a journey to it. There is nothing that is so important in the journey of success than to know that what you have is enough for the journey. All you need to do is to nurture it. Don't ever assume that you have nothing because you have something. There is no man that is born with nothing and there is no man that is born with everything. Stop blaming your financial insolvency, educational background, temperament, geographical location, economy of the country, illness, etc. Stop considering your inabilities, rather, consider your abilities. Now look at this:

If you cannot write, you can read.

If you cannot sing, you can dance.

If you cannot speak, you can listen.

If you cannot dramatize, you can watch.

If you cannot teach, you can be taught.

If you cannot invent, you can advance on already invented things.

If you cannot plant, you can harvest - Both to plant and to harvest demand energy.

Whatever you are doing, just make sure it's contributing to your journey in becoming what you desire to be. Anything you are doing is your business; in as much as it brings satisfaction in form of money and joy, and it does not deprive others from their rewards. Don't ever appreciate people more than yourself. Until you value yourself you will never amount to something in life. Until you allow your abilities to overshadow your inabilities you will never make full proof of your potentials and become all that you want to be. Why I am always motivated is that I know that there is something in me that you need. Likewise, there is something in you that I need. So appreciate it. No man can take your place in this world. You are just the original of yourself. Why not rejoice that you have a part to play in this generation. Value yourself and know that there is something in you that makes you unique. You are just you and there is no other you after you.

When you don't appreciate yourself you become vulnerable to the forces of discouragement. You make yourself a subject to every circumstance. You will be controlled by your situation. I repeat, until you accept defeat you have not been defeated. Self-defeat is the greatest defeat on earth.

Below are the ways you can grow the seed of appreciation:

(i)   Write down what you can do. Write it down on paper!

(ii)   Write down what you have. Just try to forget about what you don't have, at least for now. Think about the things that you have. For example, if you don't have money, may be you have physical strength. May be you just lost some of your properties, yet there is still something left. May be you have eaten this morning, and you have a house or a room, or you have a caring wife. You may start that business in your house, even in your car. You can never lose everything; you can only lose something. Which means that no matter what you lose there is always something left.

(iii)   Always think about things that give you joy. There is no fulfillment outside joy. You can never get better until you refuse to get bitter. No matter your misfortune, there is still something that gives you joy. Now do this: Write down those things that give you joy and read it to yourself at least once every day.

(iv)   Don't ever assume that your yesterday is better than your today. Always know that your tomorrow will be better than your today. Yesterday is gone, and tomorrow is about to come. All you have is today. And today is the womb of your tomorrow. So your excitement today will determine your placement tomorrow. Don't waste your today regretting your yesterday, anxious of your tomorrow or lamenting what you lack. Just

(v)   Learn to bury your worries of yesterday. Receive every day with joy. One destiny virus I know is called 'worry' Worry can stop you from succeeding in any business or getting to your destiny. But joy will always delay all 'delays,' discourage all 'discouragement' and hinder all 'hindrances.'

(vi)   Celebrate your position and abilities, no matter how negligible they are before others. Always thank God for what you have and where you are. Thank God for your position and your disposition. Remember that it is your disposition that determines your position. And you will never release what you have until you learn to appreciate it. So appreciate your abilities.

(Vii)   Understand that there is no 'arriver' in life; every one is a 'striver.' One man's success is another man's beginning. If you show me somebody you call a success, I will tell you about somebody that still has greater height to attain. You are not the only striver; everybody is a striver. So appreciate yourself and continue to strive. Common! You will make it!

12.   You can now turn your problems into programs

I have borrowed this statement from the late Archbishop Benson Idahosa. I believe that if there is any man that had lots of problem, he did. Going to school late in life, trying to make the government allow him build his church, trying to make the government approve his university, teaching prosperity when all we know in the Christian world was holiness, being criticized even among the Christians, the list can go on and on. Remember he was a businessman. His business was his ministry. Don't also forget that he died a multimillionaire. The name Idahosa will never end in the lips of generations to come and not only in this country but in many countries of the world. He died a success! What is the message? He succeeded because he was able to turn his problems into programs. Remember that every problem you face is a question you must answer. And you can! Just try.

Day 13 Exercise: Today you have a lot to do. You have to put these ten tools into practice. I will list them here and you will use them there. (1) Patience, persistence and perseverance (2) Don't share your problem with people that would not solve it (3) Know that no problem will last forever. (4) Be ready to do something that you did not plan for. (5) Always be ready to make a change. Yes! Plan very well. Also give room for improvising. (6) Take time to solve your problems. (7) If you cannot solve your problem then manage it. (8) Do you have a problem? Then remember your last victory. (9) Restrict your problem to yourself and God. (10) Now begin to see the good side of your problem. (11) Be joyful! (12) Start turning your problems into projects.

Day 14

Building Passion for Your Work

When you lack interest you lack excitement, when you lack excitement you lack courage, and when you lack courage you lack mental power and will power. Whatever that bores you, limits you. Enthusiasm is an essential ingredient in the school of success. You would tell better the end of someone that aspires to be an author but lacks interest in reading other people's book. Don't ever start anything because it's profitable. Do what you have passion for. You can make money in any business but you cannot stay long in a business you do not love. If you love it you will be interested in it. You will always learn more about it. You will always aspire to be like those that are already ahead of you in your profession or trade. Hatred for what you are doing can also stop you from succeeding. Love your business or job. If it is not in line with your potentials but it gives you the chance and time to nurture and release your abilities, then stay there. I repeat: Don't ever work just to live. You cannot succeed in life by working to live. Working just to earn a living is very detrimental to your destiny. Understand this: The reason why you are living is to work. It is bad to be working to live. Mike Murdock said in his book titled: The Leadership Secret of Jesus, "Work where you are celebrated and not where you are tolerated." You can never be celebrated in a business or job that you are not making maximum use of your abilities. And you cannot make maximum use of your abilities until you develop total love for whatever you are doing. If you don't love what you do, then do what you love. One thing that kills interest is the attitude of what-must-be-must-be. Let's look at that!

What-must-be-must-be

You can never succeed in life if you believe that what must be must be, because you will be carrying out your assignment without zeal. What you want is what must be. There is no limit for you on earth; you can only limit yourself. Wake up! Wake up and change your tomorrow today. Always tell yourself this: "If what I am doing is not worth dying for then it's equally not worth living for." This will erase the mentality of what-must-be-must-be and will help you to change your world. One of the weapons I used when I had nothing left with me was commitment. I knew that what I wanted is what must be, so I was doggedly committed to nurturing my destiny through knowledge. If success is your priority, then be a little more serious as I show you what I have titled the "Twelve Commandments." Just like the biblical Ten Commandments, the first gives birth to others. Keep all and be assured of success in life.

1. Love whatever you are doing

Love propels you to do more. When you love your work you will put all your efforts into it. You will learn more about it. Always be excited when you are working. Your job may be tedious but love will energize you, and you will never complain when others are complaining. Always welcome your clients with smiles. Your abilities cannot be maximized outside the atmosphere of love. NOTE: If you have strong hatred for your work, don't continue. Get another job. I repeat: If you don't love what you do, then do what you love.

2. Undermine your profit

Don't work for money but work for your future. Let money be secondary. Your profit may be below your expectation, yet don't give up. Always remember that success is not possession but contribution. It is not what you have accumulated but your donation to your world. Don't focus on your gain, rather focus on your work and be assured that harvest will come.

3. Be faithful

Unfaithfulness to man is also unfaithfulness to God. I read about a man by name Kim Woo Chong. He worked in a company for more than 7 years under a relative. He did his work with joy, was never absent from work and always took initiative on what must be done. He was a salary earner for more than seven years. He took the job as his personal business. And in 1977 after 30 years of hard work, his annual turnover was about $90 billion. He started as an employee, later became the president of Daewoo Corporation. That is the reward of faithfulness!

4. Develop yourself

Develop yourself. Oh yes! This is what engenders love. A professor was addressing some group of students. And he said, 'Now that you are going to the world to show what you know ……..' When I heard that statement, I felt I could also stand before the students to give another speech. May be my speech would go this way: 'Now that you are going to the world to know what to show …' The question is this: How can they show what they don't know? Agreed! They have acquired skills in different profession. But that is the beginning of success. They need to develop themselves. They need direction.

Every graduate needs direction because the world is a different school. The reason many graduates live in poverty is because they don't know what to show. So they end up accepting whatever the world throws on them. That is why many hate what they are doing.

One day, some group of people came to me. They explained that their leader was not giving them chance to utilize their abilities. They might be right, yet they were amazed at my response. I said to them: 'Just keep developing yourself.' Don't be in haste to manifest. Always remember that the quality of your preparation will always determine the degree of your manifestation. I remembered a day Bishop David Oyedepo was closing a service during a leadership summit, he said to us; "Don't seek to be known, seek to know" When you know you will be known. When you are fully developed, you will manifest. However,

5. Make use of every opportunity
No matter your knowledge, skill, abilities and strength, until you make use of every opportunity that comes your way, you may not succeed. Don't miss any opportunity. An old adage says: "That opportunity comes but once." That is not true anyway. Opportunity comes many times in once lifetime, but any particular one you miss will never come back again. It's gone and gone forever. So make use of every opportunity. One common factor about millionaires is that they made use of at least one opportunity to be where they are. Who knows whether the very one you miss would have given birth to success. No matter what you do, there is always a chance to take charge. So make use of it!

6. Believe you can do better
Whatever you do in life, always believe that you can do it better. Your best is never the best until you become the best. Your best is not good enough until you become all that you want to be. Stop saying; 'I have done my best' start saying, 'I can do it better.' Now look around you. Look at all the best you have done in your life, and see ways you could have done it better. Just try it again and you will be amazed at your result.

7. Always see the possibilities of things

Nothing on earth is impossible, be it good or bad, failure or success. Everything is possible if you see it that way. Believe it and see the way to make it a reality. When a thing becomes compulsory to you, your mind will begin to manufacture solution for it. That is, until your assignment becomes mandatory to you, you may not see the possibility of its accomplishment. Remember, with you and God on your side, all things are possible.

8. Always desire to be outstanding

There are two types of people on earth, those that are outstanding and those that are 'outdated.' And the difference between the two is skill. Skill is what distinguishes you from others. And skill comes from your inextinguishable quest to always do better. That is, when you refused to allow your quest for the best to be extinguished you will be distinguished. Always add value to what you are doing. Desire to be different! This will always bring out all the abilities in you and will increase your passion for your work.

9. Appreciate others

There are many reasons why you may not like your colleagues, subordinates or superiors, but there is always a reason why you should appreciate them. Always see a reason why you must love everybody that comes your way. Everybody will never be your friend, yet everybody should be loved. You can never get all that you want from people until you appreciate them. Remember that success is a collection of efforts. People bring out their best when they are appreciated, because appreciation makes one important. Don't neglect others. Value them, and they will give you all that you need to succeed in life. It's not what you do only that makes you what you want to be but what you do for others. That is, what you do and what you do for others determine what you will become. Also always appreciate things. See the good side of everything. No matter how bad a thing may be, there is always something good about it. Nothing is useless; it's only your attitude towards it that matters. Things are the way you see them, so always see good and appreciate it.

Another way to be excited in life is to always appreciate your position and also imagine your glorious destination. Your level of progress in life defines you level of success. So appreciate where you are whether it is remarkable or negligible.

10. Estimate yourself

This is the tenth commandments and of course, the most important of all. Always analyze yourself. Self-analysis is the beginning of self-realization. Socrates said: "Know thyself." In everything you do, check whether you are moving towards your stipulated goal. Somebody said, 'At least I am an average man.' But I once stated that, "It is either you are appreciating or you are depreciating, there is no stagnancy in life, it's either you are a failure or a success. There is no average person in life" Always check if you are appreciating or you are depreciating, because there is no stagnancy in life. Examine yourself always. Only you can give a correct account of yourself. Nobody can give proper estimate of you. Please understand this: Just estimate yourself monthly, quarterly, half-yearly, and yearly. It helps you to do more.

11. Be Accountable

One day, a friend of mine, Mr. Wale Adegbe introduced this key to me. He said that every Monday we would meet to account for the previous week. Each person is to explain the way he spent the previous week. During this time I spent every hour wisely. Whatever I did I would be conscious of the fact that I was accountable to somebody. Lack of accountability will ever make you to spend every hour anyhow, but if you are accountable for every hour you spend, you will spend your time working towards you goals. It helps! Get a friend, somebody you will be truthful to, meet at least once every week to account for the previous week. And always admonish each other if need be. It will help you.

12. Never Expect Commendations

Any man that expects commendation from people will never be successful in life. Always go for the contract and undermine the credit. Always understand that there must be a contract before a credit. Understand the difference between award and reward. Award may not take you anywhere but reward will bring you to your placement in life. And reward comes after the contract; award is only a credit. Do you really want to succeed in life? Then forget the credit, go for the contract. Never expect commendation from anybody. Only be committed to developing your life. And very soon you will get there!

Day 14 Exercise: Today you are expected to go through the 12 commandments carefully. Use them! Work with them. Remember, if you don't love what you do, then do what you love. It may be difficult, but you just have to. The more you love what you do; the more you will develop yourself. And the more you develop yourself; the more love you will have for what you do. Don't forget this!

Day 15
Get Up And Get Out!
Many graduates are too busy to accomplish their goals. When you see yourself being too busy to accomplish an assignment you have limited yourself in that area. To be too busy is not the same as to be working. You can be too busy and yet not working. You can be too busy yet unaccomplished. That is, active yet unproductive. That is effective, yet inefficient. Remember that it is not how active you are that matters in life but how productive you are. Not effort but result. Reader, you work smarter not harder. Also understand that in the journey of success, you do not do your best and leave the rest. You have to do your plans and leave the rest. There are three basics factors that contribute to the too Busy Syndrome: (1) Over Schedule (2) Over preparation and (3) Procrastination.

Over Schedule
This is the factor that causes the 'too busy' syndrome. Many people over schedule their assignment for the day that they end up not achieving half of it or anything at all. Other people are into this because they want to accommodate the expectation of others. Bill Cosby said, "I don't know the key to success, but the key to failure is trying to please everybody." You can never accomplish the expectation of everybody around you. Hard work is not over labour. Giving every hour a specific assignment can be termed hard work, while doing many things at a time is over labour. You cannot succeed in life, if you are involved in over labour because you will

become sick both mentally and physically. Resting revitalizes your mind for new use. Understand that it is not only how fast you are that matters, but also how far you can go matters in life. I recommend the book, The Complete Idiot's guide to Managing Your Time by Jeff Davidson.

Over preparation

This is another destiny 'virus.' Many destinies have gone to the 'home' Shakespeare described as "Undiscovered country from whose burns no traveler ever returns." The 'home' is grave. One of the reasons educated people live in poverty is because many keep acquiring certificates. They believe that if they can have their PhDs, they can live comfortably. Many destinies have been buried, because their owners were waiting for the right time to use their newly created ideas. They were very busy preparing themselves for manifestation but never attempted to manifest. What a tragedy! Many are very busy nurturing an idea that they want to implement. They need help! Please if you have one, after reading this, then help him or her. If you are one, then help yourself. Many graduates that would have started their own business are still working for others simply because they are waiting for the 'right' time to start. Indeed, the quality of your preparation determines the degree of your manifestation, yet half a loaf of bread is said to be better than none. It is better to do something half way than to do nothing. One of the greatest inscriptions I have ever read was the old Nike niche that says 'Just do it.' So just do it! I so much love the song Myles Munroe titled "It's our time." Now is your time, rise up and start that project! Get up and get out! Go to work!

Procrastination

Procrastination is not over preparation, though it gives birth to over preparation. A procrastinator may not even prepare for his assignment, though he might have the desire to accomplish it, yet, he will be postponing it. His language is always 'I will do it.' Sometimes he will say 'very soon I will do it.' But his soon never finishes until he returns to the grave and leaves his children to inherit nothing than debts. Friend, check yourself, if you procrastinate; List all the things you wanted to do at the beginning of this year, month, week or even today. How many have you done? Why didn't you do them? Is it because you believe that tomorrow is the best time? Tomorrow may be good for today but the best time for today is 'now.' Remember that now is the accepted time. Success in life demands that you make use of NOW. So get up and go to work!

Day 15 Exercise: Reader, check yourself, if you procrastinate; List all the things you wanted to do at the beginning of this year, month, week or even today. How many have you done? Why didn't you do them? Is it because you believe that tomorrow is the best time? From today, you've got to get up and go to work!

Day 16
Excuse Yourself From Every Excuses
Excuse is the factor of escape for every procrastinator. Every failure has a 'reasonable' excuse for his failure. Every excuse you create you are bound to defend. Napoleon Hill noted in his book, Think and Grow Rich, "A man's alibi is the child of his imagination." So every man is duty bound to defend his brainchild. No one ever fails without a reason for his failure. But no reason is reasonable enough to fail. Thousands of reasons for not attempting a project will never equal one reason for its accomplishment. Educated people always study the economy to know when to invest and when not to. They know when to buy shares and when not to. So they have every excuse to give for not being active for a period of time. Many graduates have every excuse for not taking a job. May be the job does not correspond with their status. And this is why many are living in poverty. If they try a thing and fail, they would give you every reasonable explanation on why they failed. Many uneducated people don't understand the economy. So they keep trying with the belief that they will make it. And they do always make it. The uneducated but informed ones know that they can make it irrespective of how bad the economy is.

I observed from experience that it's more difficult to fail than to succeed. Success is too cheap and failure is too expensive. Now consider this: You may create millions of reasons why the principles in this book will not work for you. But the only reason why it will work for you is because it is written for you. It has healed many lives and added colour to destinies. Remember that no condition is peculiar to you. My beloved reader, please excuse yourself from every excuses and you will succeed in life. Let's look at these 5 factors that give birth to excuses:

1. Shifting of blame

The factor that engenders excuses is shifting of blame. When you attribute your failure or inability to attempt a thing to another person or an event, you deny yourself the responsibility to try again. Please be responsible for your failure. Don't give any excuse for your procrastination. Accept that you are the architect of your fate, make a change and try again. For example, don't ever blame your subordinates for the business idea that failed to produce the expected result, even if one of them brought the idea. The truth is that you would have approved it before the implementation.

2. Shame

People do not want to bear the shame for failing, so they refused to take the blame. Never be ashamed of failure, for failure is the tool for success. Thomas J. Watson Sr., founder of IBM, once said, "If you want to be successful faster, you must double your rate of failure. Success lies on the far side of failure." One of the wisest men of my time, David Oyedepo, once said that, "Until they mock you, God will not make you." Many educated people are without earthly relevance today because they are ashamed to start a business or take a job that is below their standards. A wise man said, "Those who are too big to do small things are perhaps too small to be asked to do great things" No business or job is below your standard. Look at these sayings: "The man who removes mountains started by carrying away small stones." "If you must fly then learn how to creep." Friend, build a door if success refused to knock. The most reliable and authentic book in the world, the bible, admonished us not to despise the day of small things. Don't allow shame to stop you from starting that project. Start somewhere! For little is much when God is in it. Remember that if you refused to bear the shame today you will suffer the pain tomorrow. God help you!

3. Self-defeat
Shame brings self-defeat. And there is no other defeat than self-defeat. No man is defeated until he defeats himself. You are the determinant factor for your hope. It is your will to continue that brings hope again to you. Like I stated before, you may need to fail more than two times in life before you will finally succeed. And you are not defeated until you stop trying. One thing I have learnt through the hard way is that, things and people will never work for you without your cooperation. Nothing works for a defeated person. Don't forget this: self-defeat is one of the greatest obstacles to success.

4. Inferiority complex
Inferiority complex is a direct product of self-defeat. No one that has defeated himself will ever feel competent enough for a task. And until you believe that you are competent enough to tackle a task, you can never accomplish much. All the things you need to establish or advance in life will never be available. However, what is available is enough if you have confidence in yourself.

Another note: Intimidation when talking with your superiors will ever limit your abilities. God did not create anyone specially. You have equal brain cells. People are in different success categories. Some are more successful than others. Yet understand that no one is actually more useful than another. Don't ever introduce a business proposal as though you are begging for an approval. You will only end up becoming cheap. You are not a beggar; you are a businessperson. So speak like one! Understand that humility is not timidity. Wake up!

5. Mediocrity
There is no mediocrity outside inferiority complex. Mediocrity is simply the fruit of inferiority complex. No ability is not good enough for accomplishment. It is your mentality that is not sound enough to release your abilities for accomplishment. When you feel inferior you act less and you minimize your productivity. You are showing

no good quality because you believe that you are inferior, thereby limiting your abilities. Many people believe that some are destined for success than others. Somebody said; 'There is nothing I do that works.' A friend of mine once tried a business and failed, so he concluded; 'May be I am jinxed.' These are all mental pictures, which however will determine your future. No one is destined for success; and no one is also destined for failure. Wake up, friend!

Day 16 Exercise: Get a piece of paper and write your name boldly on it. Then ask yourself: Who was responsible for my last failure? Drop this book and ponder on this, at least for 10 minutes. Write the name of the person on the piece of paper. Think again: Every other time you failed, who was responsible? Write their names on that same paper. Then check all the names. Are they the same? If the names are not the same, then reread this chapter and redo this exercise.

Day 17

Conquer Indecision; Stop Wrong Decision

Every man with mediocre mentality will remain indecisive for life. Many people will never act until their relatives are in support of their decision. Any person that decides for you controls you and you will never go beyond him. The quality of your decision determines your ultimate height in life. Be decisive! Even when it is misunderstood for obstinacy, still don't give up. When Henry Ford intended manufacturing an automobile that the masses could afford, people especially his salesmen thought it would not be marketable. Some misunderstood his firmness for obstinacy but today he has left a memorial for himself. Another important thing is this: Most failures are products of wrong decision. Why is IBM not number one in the market today? They made a wrong decision. They concluded that the future of personal computers was bleak. So they decided to stick to mainframes. Today more than 50 million personal computers are sold each year. Mainframes are for few organizations. Educated people always base their decision only on research. They are very careful not to take 'unreasonable' risk. They take time to decide and they make decision based on their findings. This is one major reason many remain in poverty. In the journey of life, indecision is not worst than wrong decision. Both will always lead to failure.

Steve Job and Stephen Wozniak started Apple Computers in 1977 in their small garage. In 1994, Apple Corporation has grown to an $8 billion per year Multinational Corporation, with about 15,000 employees. What was the secret? Apple saw the future of personal computers. While IBM with all her experts (educated people), was busy supplying large, expensive inflexible computers to trained specialist in big organizations, Apple was focusing on individual users in homes, small businesses and schools. Though IBM was later forced to start producing personal computers, however, they were only playing catch-up. Don't also forget that personal computer production was one of the success secrets of Intel and Microsoft. In the school of success, one productive decision, if implemented, may change your entire life.

NOTE: To base ones judgment on research is not totally bad; however, things do always change.

Day 17 Exercise: Today you are going to take a decision about your life, family, spouse, projects, job, business, etc. Decide what you want from life. Understand that to decide means to resolve. To resolve means to make your mind up. You have wavered about that issue for so long. Today put an end to that. Understand that all through your life you will never have the best time to accomplish that project. The best time is NOW! So decide.

Day 18

Don't Think You Know; Just Learn More.

Before you make any decision in life be sure that you are not ignorant of the matter. Ability without knowledge equals futility. No matter how talented you are, ignorance will ever limit you. Reader, you can never pay the price of ignorance because it is too expensive. And the highest form of ignorance is to equate education with business knowledge. Educated people always believe that they know. They believe that studying Business Administration in the University will make you to succeed in business. That is why most of them always fail. I love the story of Ayo Arowolo - the genius behind Financial Standard, now the CEO of Invest Club Network. As a Group Editor of ThisDay, one of Nigeria's leading newspapers, he was ignorant in financial matters. He was making money, using money but didn't allow money to work for him. In Rich Dad Poor Dad, Robert T Kiyosaki, stated that the most important thing in business is cash flow. In Rich Dad's Prophecy, he said that one of the most important life skills to develop is to learn to gain control of your cash flow. Ayo Arowolo did not have control over his cash flow, until he met a millionaire that taught him necessary principles for success. Today, he is one of my best teachers. You can have your Masters in Business Administration and yet keep failing in business. It is not certificate that matters; it is practicable business ideas that guarantee success. In the world of success, knowledge is absolutely unavoidable. If you want to fail then start something you don't understand.

Let's look at the story of Dell Computers: In 1984, Austin Michael Dell started this company at the age of 19 in Texas. Before this time Apple, IBM, Digital and other companies have already taken the Personal Computers Industry. It became difficult to break the formidable barriers already built against any upstart firm. But not so with Michael Dell! What he did was to invent a new marketing and distribution system for PCs. He pioneered the direct-to-customers marketing of computers. He also discovered that customers could purchase PCs by mail or over the phone. He offered calls for technical support, a thirty-day money-back guarantee, and a free service for the first year of ownership. In 1993, his sales had exceeded $2 billion. Understand that he did not get this idea from any business school. And like Matthew j. Kiernan stated in his book, Get Innovated or Get Dead, "a single innovation or advantage is never enough", when he saw that the giants IBM, Apple, etc., have started copying his market strategy, he came up with a broader suit of products called DellWare. This product constitutes software, Pc games, modem, printers, etc. Michael Dell is not a computer guru, but a businessman. Underline this: It was knowledge that gave him the winning edge.

Day 18 Exercise: Before you start the implementation of that project, you have to know everything you need to know about it. So ask yourself: What new skill do I need to acquire in order to implement this project? What information do I need in order to start this business? Write it down and go for it.

Day 19
Learning Patience, Persistence and Perseverance.
Every great man took great time to manifest his greatness. It is certain that you should not wait until waiting becomes your habit, yet understand that patience is the factory for every greatness Nothing is easy at its raw state. Every idea must be nurtured before it could be turned into its monetary equivalent. And patience is the unavoidable 'processing factory' for every idea. The more you become impatient in life, the more costly mistakes you make. I repeat, mistakes are not bad but they delay progress. And remember that progress defines success. The more patient you are the more perfect you become. Note this: patience is not the same thing as waiting. Waiting is a posture; patience is a principle. Waiting is being passive; patience is not just being active but productive. Patience is to persevere. Patience is to persist. It means to keep trying and also to give your life adequate time to grow. So don't wait but be patient. Don't quit! Only give it time. The end of a thing is

better than the beginning, yet the beginning is always more difficult. Stop trying everything, just stay with something. Concentrate! And very soon you will get to the top!

One of the problems with our educational system is that they don't teach us certain character traits that are necessary for success in life. One of the factors in life that determine success is patience. As I stated earlier, there is a principle I have been using in every aspect of my life, it is called the Principle of the 3Ps. Patience, Persistence and Perseverance. That is it! I have stated it before, now I am going to explain how it works. Patience is the ability to deny every immediate gratification for a more viable reward. Persistent means to be consistently constant. That is steadfastness of purpose. Perseverance is the ability to be patient and persistent in the face of all odds. Not giving up no matter the enormity of the pressure. I am going to relate the story of Les Brown as I have always done to show you how this principle works. Let's go!

This is the best story that I have ever heard about patience, persistence and perseverance. He was born in an abandoned building on the floor with his twin brother Wes Brown. They were adopted when they were six weeks old, by Mrs Mamie Brown, who had very little education and financial means in a low-income Liberty City in Miami, Florida. As a young boy, Les was mislabeled a slow learner. Les was not educated. He had no education past high school. Touched by her mother's sufferings, he decided to get a job to help his mother in the family upkeep. So he went to his high school teacher and mentor, Mr. Washington. Les wanted to be a disc jockey, what we call DJ, but he had no certificate for the job, and remember that he has been labeled a slow learner.

Mr. Washington advised him to work on himself. He said to Les, "If you want to be a dick jockey, you've got be hungry. You've got to be willing to do things others won't want to do, in order to have things others won't have. You've got to go to work on yourself. Develop your mind. You don't get in life what you want, but you get what you are. Always strive to get to the top in life because the bottom is overcrowded. You've got to be hungry." He told Les to start working as a disc jockey, creating his radio format, seeking for sponsorship, developing his communication skill and personality and listening to effective communicators. Les argued that he was jobless and could not be working as a disc jockey. So Mr. Washington Reminded him again, "It is better to prepare for an opportunity and not have one, than to have an opportunity and not be prepared." After the conversation, Les went to the 'University of Self-Development", where he taught himself communication skill, created his radio format, learned how to write promotion and do jingle. When he graduated from 'USD', he went back to his mentor.

Mr. Washington reminded him again: "Remember you've got no journalism background, and you know broadcasting is a very crowded field and very competitive. You are going to face enormous rejection from everybody, but if you are hungry enough, the world will make a place for you." So he went for the job and met the Programme Director. After explaining himself and his intention, the Director asked him if he has a journalism background. And he said no. He asked him about his broadcasting experience, and he had none. You know the next action; he left without securing the job. So he went to his mentor defeated and discouraged. And his mentor said to him, "Don't take it personally. Most people are so negative, they have to say no seven times before they eventually say yes. You've got to be hungry! Go back again!" Motivated by his mentor, he went back the next day. Greeted the Director and still made his intention known to him. The Director reminded him that he had been there the previous day. Les explained that he thought that somebody was laid off or fired. The Director told him that no one was laid off or fired. So he left again without securing the job. On the third day, Les still went back to the Programme Director. Greeted him as usual and made his intention known, however, the Director interrupted with exasperation.

This was their conversation:

Director: I know what your name is, weren't you here the last three days?
days?
Les: Yes sir!
Director: Didn't I tell you 'no vacancy?'
Les: Yes sir!

Director: Then why are you here today?

Les: I don't know whether or not someone is sick or somebody died.

Director: No one is sick, no one died, no one is laid off and don't you come back here again.

The fourth day, Les still went back. Looking good as he greeted the Director, the man looked at him and asked him to go and prepare some coffee for him. He wanted to be a disc jockey and ended up as an errand boy for the disc jockey. That's good! At least he came close to his goal. I guess that was why he said, "Sometimes you have to stoop before you conquer. You've go to sacrifice before you reign." Another time, he said, "Shoot for the moon. Even if you miss it, you will land among the stars." One day the disc jockey by name Rocky Rogers was drunk while on air. So it was obvious that he would not be able to complete the show. The General Manager asked Les to call one of the DJs to complete the programme. Instead of calling other DJs, Les called his mother and told her to turn on her radio, that he was about to come on air. After waiting for about 20 minutes, he went back to the Manager, and told him that he could not find one. So he asked if Les could handle the job. That was how Les Brown became a disc jockey without any qualification. He later rose to the position of broadcast manager. Les became a community leader, three-term legislator, and a notable speaker, changing the lives of many and putting millions of dollars into his pocket. Remember I told you that the word; 'ASK' is an acronym of Ask, Seek and Knock. Les did not just ask. He did not just seek. He also knocked. Don't you think you may need to knock also, in order to accomplish that dream? Give that a second thought! Les was patient. Les was persistent. And Les persevered. I know that something is burning in your heart right now. Just get up and go back to that very place you have failed. You will succeed this time!

Day 19 Exercise: Les was patient. Les was persistent. And Les persevered. Les asked. He did seek. He also Knocked. Les was not waiting. He was only patient. The Journey of success is like building a tower, and patience is putting one brick any time you have the opportunity. Reader, are you really doing something? Or are you really doing enough? I know that something is burning in your heart right now. Just get up and start building that tower with that brick in your hand. You will succeed this time!

Day 20

Invest Your Time

Nothing delivers without patience; yet also understand that there is time for everything. Don't use your time, don't spend your time, only invest your time. Don't ever give somebody appointment and say 'you can come at any time.' Give him a specific time on a specific day. And document it in your dairy. As you wake up every morning give every hour a specific assignment before you start the day. Play while you play and work while you work. Friend, no wasted time can be retrieved. Accomplish your today, today. Don't carry it over till tomorrow. If you cannot use your hand then use your mind. Don't ever be idle.

Another area people misuse their time is by over sleeping. You cannot succeed in life by sleeping more than 8 hours everyday. A man that aspires to be great must always work at least 16 hours everyday; sleep not more than 6 hours in the night and sometimes 1 hour in the day and may be another 1 hour for relaxation. Don't sleep half of your life. Again, don't spend your productive time with your love partner. Very important! Always bear in mind that one of the greatest assets in life is not money but time. 'Time na money'

Day 20 Exercise: Today, get another piece of paper. Calculate how many years you would waste in your lifetime by wasting just 1, 2, 3, 4, 5, 6, 7 or 8 hours daily. Do the calculation yourself. It's very simple. Just multiply how many hours you waste daily by 365 days in a year. And multiply the result by 80, 90 or 100; depending on how many years you want to live. Then divide the result by 24 to know the number of days you would waste. You can still divide the result by 365 to know the number of years you would waste.

Day 21

**Look For People That Have What You
Need**.

We have discussed inferiority complex as one of destiny's viruses, but I also observe that superiority complex is an obstacle. When you feel that you are superior in a group, you deny yourself the chance to gain from others. Educated people feel superior especially among the uneducated. And that is a real problem. Learn from your superiors and also learn from your subordinates. Always remember that success is a collection of efforts and that there is no monopoly of ideas. You can't do it all! One thing I observed about most educated people is that they are ashamed of stopping a strategy that is obviously not working. You are not superior, because your subordinate may have want you need. So learn from that person no matter the level of your education.

It's more important to understand that every success in life is a collection of efforts. Lack of confidence in others will limit your growth in life. I so much love an old adage that says; "A tree can never make a forest" but I rather paraphrase it this way: "A tree is not a forest," because a tree can make a forest. Your greatness in life is completely dependable on your ability to accommodate other people's ideas. Mike Murdock once said, "What you lack is always housed in someone else." There is no monopoly of ideas, so be open to people. Check any manager that will always do everything by himself because he believes that no one can do it better, very soon he will be out of business. One of the secrets of success is your ability to reproduce yourself into others. Don't forget this!

Day 21 Exercise: Today, I want you to understand that every body is a student in the school of life. And that includes you. So you are going to search for those that have what you need in order to succeed. Don't be ashamed. Search for them. Observe them. Just learn from them. They may have the most resourceful tool that you need for your journey to the city of wealth. Don't ignore this!

Day 22

Enroll in the University of Self-Development

Back again to the story of Ayo Arowolo: Ayo read Political Science in the school, but later became the Managing Editor of Financial Standard. Why financial newspaper? Why not political? Or was it by accident? The truth is that it was the absence of the financial reporter who was on leave - that brought him to financial reporting sector. But that is not the factor behind his continuity in the industry. I am sure that the first day he went to cover the stock market would be very hectic, because till date, I still don't have a complete understanding of stock market language. Don't laugh at me. I only said the truth. This problem was enough to send him packing. But not so with Ayo Arowolo! It only made him to enroll in the 'University of Self-Development' (USD), where he had to read many hours, perhaps at night. He also met some gurus in the profession, and they tutored him. Today, he is a guru in the industry.

The greatest problem with educated people is that they exalt their certificates. And this is one of the major reasons they live in poverty. They believe that education is the same thing as information. I beg you not to mind what your advanced learner dictionary stated. If you will ever become wealthy beyond measure, I want you to undermine your certificate. Strange! But that is the truth. Just enroll in the University of Self-Development.

Jim Rohn one of the foremost American philosophers was narrating how he became a millionaire in one of the editions of his electronic magazines, and he stated, "People often ask me how I became successful in that six-year period of time while many of the people I knew did not. The answer is simple: The things I found to be easy to do, they found to be easy not to. I found it easy to set goals that could change my life. They found it easy not to. I found it easy to read books that could affect my thinking and my ideas. They found it easy not to. I found it easy to attend classes and seminars, and to get around other successful people. They said it probably wouldn't matter. .... Six years later, I'm a millionaire and they are still blaming the economy, the government and company policies, yet they neglect to do the simple basic, easy things." In The Treasury of Quotes (TTOQ), he stated, "Don't wish for less problems; wish for more skills. Don't wish for less challenges; wish for more wisdom. You must either modify your dreams or magnify your skills. You can cut down a tree with a hammer, but it takes about 30 days. If you trade the hammer for an ax, you can cut it down in about 30 minutes. The difference between 30 days and 30 minutes is skill. The key of life is to become skillful enough to do rewarding things." Now, that is a confirmation that personal development is the factory for skill, and skill is the producer of success. Not certificate, but skill. Please don't ever forget this!

I am a student of the University of Self-Development (USD). This is a school where you are the coordinator and as well as the student. You are also the examiner. The fundamental factor is choice. And in this school, there is no graduation. This is a school with no specific building. It takes place in your car, room, work place, at beach, in the church, in the day and mostly at night. It's a school where learning is preferred to schooling and skill replaces certificate. Here, I think I should tell you something about myself: I gave myself to learning. I can use almost all the Microsoft Office packages and all versions, including 2003 version. That is, Word, Excel, Access, Outlook, Publisher, Front Page, Power Point, One Note, InfoPath, etc. On graphics, I can use Corel Draw, Corel Photo Paint, Adobe Photo Shop, Adobe Image Ready, Macromedia FreeHand, Macromedia Fireworks, Corel RAVE, Microsoft GIF Animator, Ulead Cool 3D, etc. On accounting, I can use MYOB, I am not too good with Peachtree. On web development, I am still a learner; however, I can use MS Front Page, Macromedia Dreamweavers, code HTML, I have also designed few websites. I can also use Macromedia Flash. I am still learning programming language like JAVA. I also use Adobe Page Maker. I did computer Engineering and Networking. Last year, I did a '5 in one' training program, which constitutes: Computer Engineering, Networking, CCNA, VSAT and VOI configuration. I am also a writer and a public speaker, but I do not have any journalism background. I want you to understand that I did not acquire these few skills from any University. I acquired them from the School of Personal Development what I call the University of Self-Development. I started my speaking career speaking to my students at IMT Computers. I made it a duty to be giving them inspiring speeches every morning before the normal lectures starts. I also started to write by writing for my church magazines. And I have written many books that are yet to be published. Among them is a great book under the Missing Course series that will be published later this year, titled, "Wealthy Barber Poor Professor." This is one book that can turn a dullard into a financial guru. I guarantee you that! If you have read my first book under the Missing Course series, titled, "If You Want To Be Wealthy, Don't Be A Graduate?" and you are reading this one now, then you know what I can offer. But if you want to read the first chapter for free, then send me an email. Don't forget, my email address is uyanwanneraphael@yahoo.com

I started teaching on relationships by helping the youths to solve their personal relationship problems. In one of my books co-authored by Bose Shodeinde, titled; 'What Every Man Must Know About A Woman', you will discover the products of my encounter with young people.

I have just told you part of my story. But what is the keyword? Practice! The fact is this, I know that I am going to major in writing and speaking, however, I want you to understand that practice is the fundamental principle for self-development. For example, my budget for books and seminars is too small, so I supplement with practice. And it's actually working for me. Before you start that project or business, please prepare, practice, practice and practice. If you intend to start a publication, you may need to work in a publication company first. Don't ever undermine this!

Day 22 Exercise: What you are going to do today is that you will start making enquiry on how to acquire a specialized skill. Sure, you cannot acquire it in a day, but you will start the journey today, if you have not started. There are many skills you can acquire on the Internet. And they are for free. If you want to learn any of these skills, then send me a mail. Skills like e-publishing (electronic publishing), web development, software development, using application packages, computer engineering, graphics, etc. You can also learn many other skills on the Internet for just a token fee. But if you cannot get what you want to learn on the Internet, then register with any school or organization that offers it. You are going start making the enquiry about it today. And after today make it a duty to always acquire at least one specialized skill every 2 years. You will be glad you did!

Day 23

Conquer That Atom of Greed

There was a man who lived in the twenties. His name was Arthur Barry. He was a man who gained international recognition as a jewel thief. He was an unusual jewel thief, a remarkable one of all time. One night he was caught during robbery and was shot three times. Like every apprehended robber, he exclaimed, "I'm never going to do this any more." However, he later escaped. But the law of Seed Time and Harvest Time hunted and fetched him out. A jealous woman implicated him and he served an eighteen-year sentence. He wasted eighteen productive years in prison. When he was released he kept his word. He never stole again. As a once notorious man, one day, reporters all over the country came to interview him. One of the reporters asked him the most penetrating question of all, "Mr. Barry, you stole a lot from wealthy people during your years as a thief, but I'm curious to know if you will remember the one whom you stole the most?" And Barry replied, "That is easy, the man from whom I stole the most was Arthur Barry, I could have been a successful businessman, a baron on Wall Street and a contributing member of the society but instead I choose the life of a thief and spent two-third of my adult life behind prison bars."

The time and effort used in stealing from others is greater than what it takes to overcome poverty in life. You may not be a jewel thief like Arthur Barry, but do you cheat others to succeed? There are many routes to failure but the shortest of them all is to cheat. Are you a robber? Understand that you rob yourself the most any time you rob others. To rob means to deny someone of what belongs or would belong to him or her, either by intimidation or manipulation.

If you are a student in any university, polytechnic or college of education in this nation, you know that many lecturers always involve themselves in this. And that is why they remained in poverty.

How many people have you denied what belongs to them in the name of trying to succeed in life? Cheating to succeed will deny you the dignity that is labour. Don't cheat anyone whether the person is your subordinate or your family member. Better still; don't steal from your customers. The journey of success is a long one but integrity is the determinant for continuity. I state it again: Integrity is the sole of business, not dignity. Competence can never replace character. A man of integrity knows that one client is as important as another. He also knows that cheating doesn't last long, because very soon the people will discover. He knows that the content of a package is more important than the container. As you will discover in the next segment, you can sell more by packaging a product beautifully and differently, yet packaging is most times deceitful. People can buy because of the package but they will keep buying because of the value they derive from the product. You can obtain customers by your packaging but you retain them because of the genuineness of your products. Sell what you can buy and do what you say. Integrity is consistency. Integrity is trustworthiness. Everyone is climbing the ladder of success but whoever climbs because he is stronger will soon fall because of loneliness. One of the ways you can be failing without knowing is to be manipulating others for your selfish gain. If you hire somebody to work for you, always pay the person as at when due. Every extra time used for you must be paid for, either in cash or in kind. Don't ever motivate your workers because you want to make more profits. That is manipulation. Inspire others but never manipulate. I still maintain this philosophy that, "Manipulation is making others to do what you want. Inspiration is helping others to do what they want." Work with this. It will help you. Remember that this not in our school syllabus.

Day 23 Exercise: Have you ever robbed others of what belongs or would belong to them, either by intimidation or manipulation? Have you ever motivated your workers in order to make more profit? Have you ever used others to climb the ladder of success? Do you sell what you cannot buy? Today you have to change. Resolve to stop.

This will pay you at the long run. I promise you! You may not be able to stop everything at once. Just begin somewhere.

Day 24

Start Producing and Implementing Ideas

Everyone has an idea but not everyone has profited from his or her ideas. It is certain that every multinational company started as an idea in the heart of someone. I have always stated that what you cannot complete in you mind; you cannot also complete with your hands. The products of thinking are ideas. Anyone can manufacture one, but not everybody can nurture it to its productive stage. Your idea is like your baby; it can suffer malnutrition or even die of hunger. Your idea is your bouncing baby boy; you've got to feed, train, and love him until he is matured enough to pay you back. All through the polytechnic or university, you will never learn how to produce and nurture your ideas to fruition. If you are a graduate, then you understand what I mean. And that is why many graduate suffer so much in life. No one becomes wealthy without knowing how to produce, present, process, practice an idea and then profit from it.

There are five important stages of every idea: Production, presentation, processing, practicing and profiting. Now, before I explain these stages, I want you to understand what an idea is:

What is an idea?
From series of researches, there are two ways to manufacture an idea. One is through synthetic imagination, and the other through creative imagination. Synthetic imagination is simply thinking of how you can modify an existing idea for maximum productivity. Every success starts with an idea. It can be an existing idea, yet when modified, can lead to success in life. Always think on how you can do it better and differently. Look at this: The first person that started the sachet water business, what we call pure water - was not the manufacturer of the idea. Since the advent of refrigerator, market women had been selling 'pure water.' The difference is that they couldn't package it; they only used nylon bags. Mark Andreessen,

the Co-founder of Netscape, was not the person that created World Wide Web. Tim Berners-Lee did. Also remember, that Tim was not the manufacturer of Internet concept. The story of Jeff Bezo will explain it better:

As the vice-president of D. E. Shaw, a financial institution, Jeff Bezo was asked to give the statistic of the Internet. This was 1994 when only academicians and computer scientists use the Internet to send text messages to their colleagues. Bezo was surprise to discover that the Internet was growing at a very fast rate. It became obvious to Bezo that in the near future, millions of people would be using the Internet. He began to think on what to sale on the Internet. He made an inescapable conclusion that books would be easy to deliver to customers all over the world by mail. He had to resign from his well-paid job. In 1995 he lunched Amazon, which has over a million titles. He started with $1 million. Don't tell me that that was a big money to start with. He managed to get the money through contacts from Wall Street. In 1998 their turnover was $1 billion. In 1999, the company was estimated at $22 billion, and Bezo's share was estimated at $9 billion. Jeff Bezo was not the original owner of World Wide Web concept. He only saw how to become a millionaire through the Internet. And he did.

When I wrote my first story for a television programme, I went to a brother, Emeka Igozurike, for help. As we were going to present the script to a programme manager, he said to me, "knowledge is stolen." I wondered what the message was all about. So he began to tell me his story. This brother did marketing in school and later, became an advertising agent. According to him, it was where he was working as a marketer, that he 'stole' the knowledge of advertising. He later worked as an advertising agent in two companies, and later became a CEO of an advertising company. He 'stole' the idea. One lesson from his story is this: An idea can be borrowed. You can travel to a place, discover something, and go back to your country to try it. You don't need to manufacture one before you succeed in life. Just modify one to suit your project.
Another kind of imagination is creative imagination. Doing something in a new way is not creativity. Please bear with me for contradicting your belief. I have intentionally defined creativity as

invention. Creative imagination means manufacturing ideas. That is inventing things in your mind - things that have never existed before. The Candescent light never existed before Thomas Edison. Electricity never existed before Michael Faraday; Coca-Cola never existed before Asa Candla (even if somebody sold the idea to him), etc. Whatever you see today was birthed by creative imagination. Somebody invented them through creative imagination. You can invent something also. Whatever may be your potential; you can do what no one has done.

But whether creative or synthetic imagination, one thing is certain, ideas rule the world. Just use your brain and gain access to your placement! A wise man said, "Wealth is the product of man's capacity to think." I totally agree with him, because it is the use of the brain that brings gain. It is wits that create wealth. It is the use of the sense that determines your level of your success. Forgive me, because I have borrowed these last three statements from David Oyedepo. Just understand that sense brings success. Until you are able to manufacture ideas or modify existing ones, you may not unlock your abilities and become what you want to be. Every success is birthed by an idea. Think of this: When you manufacture an idea, you will begin to produce what the world needs and people have no other choice than to buy from you. If you know what I don't know, you produce what I don't have, and I have no other choice than to buy from you. Though an idea has no value in its raw state, yet every great business started with an idea. No matter how talented or educated you are, it takes an idea to manifest. Knowing what you have is one thing, knowing what to do with what you have is another thing. An idea shows you what to do with what you have. We go to school to acquire a skill (though many graduates have certificate but lack the skill), yet understand that it is one thing to have a skill, it's a different thing to know how to make money with your skill. Educated people are very conscious of what they have. But not all know what to do with what they have. And I believe that this is why many still suffer. It is not what you have that matters but what you do with what you have. It is not just knowing what to do, but doing what you know. According to E. W. Kenyon, "Make the brain work, though it will sweat yet make it work." That is, think! Think! Wake up as we look at the five stages of ideas:

Production: This is a stage when a thought just comes into your mind while you are reading, thinking or even working. It comes even when you are driving or taking your bath or doing any other thing. What differentiates an idea from ordinary thought is documentation. Written thoughts are ideas. Once it comes into your mind, write it down. Understand that what will enhance your mental power are motivational books and tapes. Don't ever forget this! Another thing is this: To get a good idea, you have to manufacture many ideas. Then filter them.

Presentation: This is the most delicate stage. This is when you present your idea to your boss, your father, your best friend, your wife, your pastor or your intimate friend. Don't be surprise if no one buys your idea. Some may even share their bad experiences in order to discourage you. But experience is not expertise. If you allow them, they will discourage you. I have been there! H. E. Jansen said, "The man who wins may have been counted out several times, but he didn't hear the referee." I know what it means if your own pastor refuse to allow you to implement an idea. Sometimes it is the person you thought would help you with the start-up capital that may discourage you. Many people have allowed their ideas to die at this stage. One hard truth is this: No one can discourage you, if you refuse to be discouraged.

Processing: This stage requires isolation. You may need to wake up at night to think. This is when you begin to modify the ideas. You begin to make it practicable, removing some things and adding other things.
Practicing: This stage takes place with the processing stage. That is, you modify and as well implement. This is another risky stage. Be very careful but don't be too careful. This stage translates an idea to its monetary equivalent or makes one to loose his fortune. This stage brings temporal misfortune or permanent fortune. Don't forget that it was the risk Asa Candla took by buying a piece of paper with written ideas and a kettle for $500 that translated to Coca-Cola. May be you've not read or heard of Asa Candla, but sure you've seen a Coca-Cola depot or truck. That is someone's idea and risk!

Profiting: This is the most fascinating stage. Now, you are beginning to enjoy the fruits of your ideas. Proper processing and practicing of your ideas also sustain this stage. You have to keep modifying and implementing your ideas for it to keep producing profits. This is when you may need to change the title of a book and not the content in order to sell more. You may need to change the name of a product or manufacture the product in another form to increase your profits. You may need to change the name of your company. You may also sell a product or provide a service in different ways. You can have a tape version of a book. You can also have it in CDs. I am just giving some examples. Begin to use your brain now!

Day 24 Exercise: Today, you are to create an idea book. The book should be so small that you can carry it anywhere you go. Anytime an idea comes into your mind, just write it in the book. Write as many ideas as you can. Present the ideas to your friends. I mean your friends not your acquaintances. Then consider their opinions but be very careful. Don't allow any of them to stop you. Now, keep modifying the ideas. Remember, to have a good idea you must have many ideas.

Day 25

Get Up And Set That Goal

A life without a goal will be void of significance. You can survive without a goal. You may also be stable without a goal. But you cannot succeed without a goal. Better still, you cannot be significant without a goal. A man without a goal will never make a mark on earth. Without a goal you can never be relevant to your generation. Goal is the fuel for fulfillment. The live wire of every success in life is goal. It naturally guarantees your access to the world of excellence. It engenders the motivating power for greatness. Every outstanding success is a function of an accomplished goal. It takes goals to reach an enviable height of triumph in your pursuit in life. Goals are the documentation of what you want to do, how and when you want to do them. Every goal must be simple, realistic, written, flexible and specific in nature. The only problem is that our schools have no course that major practically in goal setting. This is the reason many educated people make serious financial mistakes, because they cannot set financial goals.

Simple
Every goal must be simple, not complicated. If it is complicated, then break it down to smaller goals. And focus on one at a given time. For example, if you want to own an automobile company, you may need to start with a vulcanizing shop. You may need to start by selling second-handed automobile spare parts. All you need to do is to start planning on how to own a vulcanizing or automobile workshop. Remember that focus is the key to achievement.

Realistic:
Then be realistic! Be able to differentiate a goal from a dream. Your dream may be to build chains of industries across the entire world. Another question is what industry? You said cosmetics. That is still a dream. You have perfume, powder, cream, etc. You said cream. That is still a dream. What type of cream? Have a big dream but have a realistic goal. Wishful thinking is not faith. I believe that having a realistic goal is very important. It is also unrealistic stating a goal like making =N=10 million in a year when your overall income per month is below =N=50,000. It is better to exceed your goals than to set unrealistic goals that you cannot achieve.

Written:
Any goal that is not written is mere wish. And wishes don't materialize. Goals should be written for motivation. Written goals are motivating factors for every achievement. Before I started learning and reading about goals, my father taught me many things about this. As a part-time farmer, he would always use our calendar as his jotter. I believe that it was easier for him that way because of the dates he would always mark on the calendar. He would always mark dates for planting of yam, cassava, etc; Dates for clearing the weeds, etc. Till all the products are harvested and another year comes, our calendar would always be a mess. And he would always tell his harvest before it comes. Except for one bad year, he rarely missed any of his targets. I have read many great books about this

topic, but I have clearly stated this strategy because it's working for me. Do you have a goal? Please write it down!

Flexible:
Like I stated before, whatever that motivates you can later begin to bore you. That is why your goals should be flexible to the extent that it can be modified. You see, dreams are to be magnified; goals are to be modified. There are things you cannot control, e.g. Power supply, strike, sickness, etc. These circumstances may make you not to meet your targets. That is not defeat. That is delay. You have to amend and continue. It will only cost you an extra sheet of paper.

Specific:
Being specific about your goals is not just being realistic. It's not just about knowing what to do. It's about stating when to accomplish each goal. It is about when not what. Every goal without a date of accomplishment lacks motivating power. Don't just state what you want to do. Also be specific about the date you want to accomplish each goal. Don't be discouraged if you fail to accomplish any of your goals at the stipulated date. Just modify it and work toward its accomplishment. Remember; always set simple, specific, realistic, flexible and written goals.

Day 25 Exercise: Now that you have some good ideas you want to implement. You are going to specify how you will implement the best of them all. Let what you want to do be very simple, written and flexible. You can use your idea book. But be realistic. Let whatever you want to do be achievable. Then specify the date you want accomplish it.

Day 26
Avoid Distractions; Allow Opportunities.

Distractions always come as opportunities. It takes commitment to differentiate between the two. It is not all offers that are opportunities, some are distraction, and they come to test your level of commitment. Educated people always see themselves as having greater opportunities than the uneducated ones, however, many don't understand the difference between an opportunity and a distraction. Many are being drifted all through their lives and would always wind-up broke. One major thing I love Ayo Arowolo for, is his commitment to his purpose on earth. It really baffled me when I learnt that he refused about five fantastic offers, most especially an offer to work in a bank and be earning =N= 250,000, with free accommodation and official car, at a time he was earning just =N= 12,000. Don't tell me that he was able to provide for the entire family with =N=12,000. This means that one of the major problems he had was lack of money. And he rejected an 'opportunity' like this. So what was his secret? He was committed to his goals. He had an unflinching desire to accomplish his dream. He could tell an opportunity from a mere distraction. I love him! I have been there, so I know what it means.

Many educated people actually have dreams but are not committed to their goals. Your dream is your vision. Know the end of your journey so that you will always be motivated. Alexander Hamilton said, "Those who stand for nothing falls for anything," David Jordan also said, "The world will stand aside to let you go, if you know where you are going." So know where you are going. Just drop this book and think of this: The end of a man leaving his house in the morning, after taken his bath, with expensive suit yet not knowing where to go. I think the summary of the story is frustration. Until you design where you are going to, you may not leave where you are. I love this slogan always used by the architects that: "The client shapes the structure, from then on the structure shapes the client." As you have determined your goal, from now upward your goal should determine what you do. Goals motivate. It breeds consistency and it makes everyday joyful for you. Don't only set goals for yourself but set 'big goals.' Let your dream be big enough and your goals realistic enough to keep you alive all the days of your life. Say this prayer:

"Disturb me O Lord when I am too well pleased with myself,

when my dreams have come true because I dream too small,
when I have arrived in safety because I sailed to the shore.

"Stir me O Lord, to dream and dare more boldly,
to venture on the wilder seas,
where storm shall show thy mastery,
where losing sight of land I shall find the stars.

"In the name of Him who has pushed back the horizons of our hope,
and invited the brave to follow Him." Anonymous

Again, if you have designed a 'big goal', the next thing is direction. Most educated people don't seek for direction. They believed that their experiences in the school are enough for the journey of success. You need direction! For example, if you are traveling from Ibadan to Lagos (assuming you live in Nigeria) Lagos becomes your dream. Since you cannot just appear in Lagos, you must travel. So traveling becomes your assignment or purpose. Another question is: How do you travel: By air, sea or land? If land, then which road? What is the shortest distance? And is it safe? All these questions constitute your directions. In this book you must have discovered some directions but I want to show you the easiest way to get directions. Let's look at our illustration above: Since you don't know Lagos and you want to travel to Lagos, what you will do is to look for somebody that either lives in Lagos or that had traveled to Lagos recently. From this person you can now acquire the necessary information. Look for those that have succeeded in life. Those that have achieved the goals you intended to achieve or those that are at least closer to your goals. No matter how unique your goals are, somebody somewhere must have accomplished something that is similar to it. Don't doubt this; just believe it. Receive directions from those that are ahead of you in life. There is one major way this can be accomplished, and that is by mentorship. The next section will guide you.

Day 26 Exercise: Hey, that new job you want to get, is it really in line with your dream on earth? Or don't you have a dream? May be I should put it this way: Do you have a long-term goal? Do you know what you will become at the end of your journey on earth? You must know where you are going. Because failure to do this will make you to accept where you are. And not just that. You will also accept whatever that comes your way as an opportunity. Reader, there are distractions out there disguised as opportunities. It takes knowing what you want from life to differentiate between the two. Now that you have documented your dream, don't ever modify it unless it's somebody else dream. Modify your goals not your dream.

Day 27

Now, You Need a Mentor

Success in life requires that you have a mentor. Your mentor is any person that you go to for advice, who must be ahead of you. Some authors see a mentor as somebody that is either below or ahead of you or even your colleague. But in this book I have specifically stated that your mentor is somebody that is ahead of you in life, not in terms of age but in advancement or achievement. I prefer older people. Not somebody that is below you or your colleague. Like I always say, all men on earth are not equal. One thing I observed is that most educated people don't have mentors. Even those that have only make educated people their mentors. If you will ever become all that you are destined to become in life, then you must make sure that your mentor has not just schooled but has also made life a school. Your mentor must be a student of life. He or she must also have a mentor. Mentorship is a place for practical knowledge. It is a place where you discover what has worked for others, in order to make it work for you.

For example when I read Bishop David Oyedepo's books, he often makes reference to men like Kenneth Harggin, Kenneth Copeland, Gloria Copeland, Vincent Normal Pearl, Smith Wigglesworth, E. W. Kenyon, etc. I discovered from one of his books that Kenneth Copeland got some inspirations from Kenneth Harggin and Harggin from Smith Wigglesworth. Bishop David Oyedepo received the secrets of financial breakthrough from Gloria Copeland's book, while I received the mystery of financial prosperity from two of his books: Breaking Financial Hardship and Understanding Financial Prosperity. I recommend these two books for you.

Let it be settled in your heart that we are of different categories. So note those that are ahead of you and chose a mentor. You may not really need to see all your mentors; you can acquire information through their books. However, you must have one or two you can always go to for advice.

Mentorship increases your rate of progress and minimizes the number of mistakes you make in life, because you learn from your mentors sermons and scars. You learn from his success and also his failures. This shortens your journey to success. The easiest way to get what you need from your mentor, especially if you are with him or her, is to serve him. Yes! Stewardship is the pathway to success. Remember that greatness in life is not by nature but by nurture. You do not just assume it; you consciously nurture yourself into it. And stewardship is a compulsory ingredient. Learn to serve before you make others to serve you.

There are three ways you must follow in order to gain from your mentor: (1) Get informed (2) Get motivated and (3) Get imparted.

Get Informed.
Allow your mentor to deposit into you all the necessary information. Make use of every opportunity you have, and acquire from him as much knowledge as you can. Put everything you discovered, and the ones that are delivered to you into your head. This is the first step.

Get Motivated
Be inspired by your mentor. Allow him to motivate you. Love him and ignore every criticism or personality flaws. Every time you are listening to his tapes or reading his books or you are having face-to-face conversation with him, be motivated for action. Until you value your mentor you may not apply all the principles he will be unveiling to you. Always see him as a success. Mike Murdock described mentorship as "Acquiring perfect knowledge from an imperfect man." In his book 'Towards Excellence in Life and Ministry' Bishop Oyedepo narrated his story with late Archbishop

Benson Idahosa. There is something that fascinates me every time I read this book: Idahosa imparted him because he didn't come to him as a colleague but as a servant. Today the result is undeniable. Irrespective of your belief, you cannot undermine the part of mentorship in life. Please ignore your mentor's imperfection if you really want to command the same result like him or her.

Get Imparted
This is the third step and the most important. Make sure that your mentor imparts your life. Apply every key you discover from him or her. I am not talking about imitation but impartation. You can only imitate somebody for a while but impartation is forever. However, if it means to imitate your mentor, then do. Imitate him or her. You cannot be imparted and not produce the same result as your mentor. I strongly believe in impartation because I have seen the result in my life. Look for people that are ahead of you in life and allow them to impart your life. My beloved reader, if it were possible, I would persuade you or rather plead with you to follow these simple yet profound principles in life. The ladder to your placement in life is conspicuously positioned. And you must carefully climb until you arrive at your destination. The ladder I am showing you in this book has no substitute. So make use of it!

For you to be imparted you must be able to differentiate these two words: adaptation and adoption. You must be able to adapt to every idea you receive from your mentor before you adopt them into your life. There must be adaptation before adoption. There are principles that your mentor must have integrated into his or her life that contributed immensely to his or her success. These principles may need some refinement before you begin to integrate them into your life, especially if you got the principles from their books or tapes. Try to adapt to every key you receive before you apply it totally into your life. If you still do not understand, then let me explain with this example:

Many educated people always come to me with some books, and say, 'Ralph, the principles in this book will only work in America not here in Nigeria.' My response has always been that if you can adapt before you adopt them, they will definitely work in Nigeria. For example, if you are used to two hours reading every day and your mentor suggest that you begin to read for six hours daily. If you start it this way, it will definitely be burdensome to you. You can start with three hours, if you are okay with three hours, then start for four hours and so on. When information is crudely integrated it can lead to frustration and will end in futility. Try to re-program your system to accept every principle before you integrate it fully into your life. Remember, most of the books we read in this country are written by foreigners. Sure! Most of them don't really understand our economy. However, the secrets of wealth have not changed. Only try to adapt before you adopt them.

Day 27 Exercise: If you have read my book under the Missing Course series, titled, 'If You Want To Be Wealthy, Don't Be A Graduate?' and you understand the difference between being rich and being wealthy, then write down the names of all the wealthy people you know. And choose one or two as your mentor. Now make that call or send that mail, informing them that you've chosen them as you mentors. Or if need be, take one of them out for a dinner or lunch. Be open. Ask questions and take the answers.

Day 28

Take The Responsibility And Design Your Life

"When you ignore your responsibility you become a liability." (David Oyedepo) God cannot do for man what man can do for himself. Give life all that it takes, and soon you'll get all that it offers. One of the things that it takes to succeed in life is planning. Remember the old saying that, 'failure to plan is planning to fail.' Having goals and dreams without plans is wishful thinking or daydreaming. Also planning without goals and dreams is total nightmare. The planning I refer to here is not as in town planning. No! It is different from forecasting. Yes! It is different from those courses you have in the school. It is not in the school syllabus. Most educated people are not trained planners. Planning in a simple term means a proper documentation of how to use what is available to get what seems impossible.

Don't waste your time daydreaming. That is not planning. Every planner is a time investor. That is, it takes time to reason. It takes time to plan. Sit down and reason how you can use what is available to do what seems impossible. At the root of every failure is time-abuse. Winners invest their time planning; losers spend their time daydreaming. All things are possible to those that plan. Remember J. A. Holmes said, "Never tell a young person that something cannot be done. God may have been waiting for centuries for somebody ignorant enough of the impossible to do that thing." Nothing is impossible for a resourceful planner. And planning becomes resourceful when it is based on realities and it's documented. That is plan with what you have and write your plans. For example, don't plan to rent a shop of =N=100,000 when all you have is =N=50,000. That is not faith. Please forgive me if I am contradicting you belief. I have made that mistake. The next segment will explain what faith is all about. Where you want to be at the end of your journey on earth is your dream. All that you want to accomplish in order to actualize your dream are your goals. How to use what is available to accomplish your goals and then actualize your dream is your plan. So planning has no substitute! Even praying cannot take the place of planning. You don't delegate planning to another person. I warn you!

Day 28 Exercise: Where you want to be at the end of your journey on earth is your dream. All that you want to accomplish in order to actualize your dream are your goals. How to use what is available to accomplish your goals and then actualize your dream is your plan. Do you have a plan? If your answer is 'yes' then continue reading. If not, then start today. Get a file and label it 'Planning.' Write your plans on separate sheets, so that they can be easily modified. Put all the sheets in the file. Review and modify them as necessary.

Day 29

You've Got To Build And Fuel Your Faith

Faith is built in the mind, expressed through the mouth and practiced with the hands. I want to start this topic with the mind. The reason God gave you a mind is for you to think. Thinking simply means reasoning. It means using your mind. Pastors, Philosophers, Psychologists, Therapists, even the system of metaphysics agreed that 'thoughts are things' Man is a product of what he thinks. Marcus Aurelius puts it this way, "A man's life is what his thought makes of it" One of the wisest men, Ralph Waldo Emerson said, "A man is what he thinks about all day long" Even the most reliable and scientific book, the bible attest to this, "For as a man thinks in his heart, so is he." So, in the journey of success, you can never travel beyond your thought. If you think success you see success. If you think failure you see failure. Now you may be tempted to ask a question like this: But I think about my aspiration yet I keep failing? Thinking success is not allowing the word, 'success' to be in your mind or occasionally casting your mind on your aspirations. It is not what you consciously allow to flash through your mind. The actual you, is what you habitually imagine to be - The picture of your life that resides in your mind.

In his book, 'Alive in Christ', Charles Price said, "You are not what you think you are, you are what you think." This statement holds the difference between success and failure, educated and informed, rich and wealthy. Let me put it this way: 'You are not what you think you are but rather, you are what you think.' In this section, we are not going to look at thinking as manufacturing ideas to be processed into its monetary equivalent, but rather the attitude of allowing your future to reside in your mind. The mind is divided into two: conscious and subconscious mind. And in this section, we will explore on the power of the subconscious mind. What you think you are is manufactured in your conscious mind, but what you really are is what is in your subconscious mind. I agree totally with Charles Price: You are what you think, not what you think you are, because what resides in your subconscious mind controls your life.

Many want to become something yet think failure. Failure cannot produce success. Error cannot produce good. Your subconscious mind is the factory for your future. It controls you and what controls you determines your future. If failure resides in you because of your past experiences, you can never succeed in life. You are not what you think you are, you are what you think. Let's explain this statement with this complicated yet profound illustration:

Let's assume success is a fruit for a minute. Then every fruit has a seed. The seed of success is first planted in your subconscious mind, before it begins to manifest. Now look at this: A mango tree is not a mango tree because it grows mango, but it grows mango because it's a mango tree. Even when it is not matured to bear fruit, it is still a mango tree. There is a general saying that "A tree is known by its fruit," but this statement is not always correct. Your fruit is what you do. You are not what you do but you only do what you are. Read that last statement again. Attitude is what you are. Action is what you do. Your attitude determines what you do. Your action only reveals what you are. What you do shows what you are, but what you are determines what you do. And what you think is what you are.

Let's see it in another way: Your character is what you are. Your personality is what you do. And understand that your personality can be different from your character. You are not your personality but you are your character. And your character is a product of what you think habitually. What you think you are is your personality, but what you really are is your character. So what you are is what you think and what you think is what you actually become. I know you understand it now. But if not, then go through it again.
You can consciously think success and yet not succeed. It is what you think subconsciously that determines your future. Unless your thinking becomes habitual it will never be planted in your subconscious mind. The word habitual implies that it becomes your attitude not your action. Your subconscious mind is very powerful, yet vulnerable to manipulation. You can manipulate your subconscious mind by planting seed of success into it. And the only way to do this is by habitually imagining your future. Write your future bold on a piece of paper, read it, talk it, pray it, see it, believe it until you are becoming it in your mind and you will become it physically. When you read, talk, pray, see, and believe your tomorrow today, your subconscious mind will accept you that way. Though it may take days or weeks; may be months, to plant seed of success in your subconscious mind. Yet if you do, you will surely

be. Talk and think success until it becomes your habit. Once you are a success (in your mind) you will definitely succeed. If you become what you want to be in you mind; it will definitely materialize in the physical.

In designing your future, you must plan your work and work your plan. Many plan their works but very few work their plans. One of the ways to work your plan is by habitually thinking about your future and your strategies. Many people believe that working your plan means doing something physically to carry out your arrangements for a specific assignment. That is not correct. Work starts from the mind. I repeat, whatever you cannot complete in your mind, you cannot also complete with your hands. Even if you start you will fail. May be that is why you have been failing in that project. Now try this: After mapping out strategies for accomplishing your assignment, visualize its accomplishment in your mind. Do this until you are overwhelmingly aware of the joy of its accomplishment. Do it until something tells you that 'you are unstoppable.' And in reality nothing can stop you. Just try this, and you will be amazed at your results. This is the beginning of faith!

Here Comes Faith!
Faith in God guarantees your access to God's blessings, yet this is just a fundamental key to accomplishment. Faith in God becomes futile when you do not have faith in yourself. It is one thing to know that God is what He says He is and that He can do what He says He can do. It is a different thing to also believe that you are what He says you are and you can do what He says you can do. It is a different thing entirely to know that you can become what you want to be and that you have all it takes to become what you want to be.

Have faith in God. Also have faith in yourself. Believe in yourself as you also believe in God. Until you believe in yourself you cannot become what you want to be. Let's see the difference between faith in God and faith in you in the following paragraphs:

Many people believe in God. They believe that God will prosper them. They pray, fast and keep waiting for a 'deliverer', somebody that God will send to favour them and change their destinies. Some believe that someday they will win a lottery. Some also believe that their future is in God's hand. Some tried in the past and failed, now they concluded; 'By strength shall no man prevail'; 'It's not by power, it's not by might'; 'Except the Lord build the city they labour in vain that build it'; 'It is God that gives power to make wealth'; etc. Others went further to say: 'At God's appointed time I will succeed'; 'God's time is the best' All these statement connotes faith in God, yet many waited till their death. Is God unfaithful?

Faith in God is the only key that guarantees your access to God's blessing, yet not all that claimed to have faith in God have succeeded in life. One day I was privileged to encourage some group of people exclusively Prayer Warriors (Intercessory group) and I talked on 'Determining your appointed time.' I was emphasizing that you are the one to determine when you will be blessed and become a success in whatever you do. Immediately I finished my message, there was division in the group. But 'God determines when and who to bless' a lady complained. Now the question is: Is God partial?

Faith is the master key to God's treasure house. Faith in God is a fundamental principle to accomplishment in life, yet it is never an automatic guarantee for fulfillment. It only marks the beginning of your journey of success. Success demands that you also have faith in yourself. Know that now is the time for accomplishment; also know that you are the person to bring it to pass, not God. You are the one to determine your rate of progress in the journey of success. You are the one to determine the colour of your destiny, not God. And this is birthed by faith in you. Believe in yourself. Believe in your abilities. Don't give any excuse. Just believe in yourself. Believe that nothing is impossible to you with God on your side.

Fuel Your Faith!
If before reading this book you have already known what you want to become. Good! If not then put the exercises in this book into practice. So write it down, if you have not written it down. Friend, please know where you are going. Know your end before you start.

Create your end. Always see your end. "You can never leave where you are, until you decide where you want to be." (Mike Murdock) Think about this: Can you leave your house for a journey without knowing where you are traveling to? If you don't know where you want to be, how will you know when you arrive? The road to nowhere is always frustrating.

Your end is your destination - final address. I repeat, if you don't know your end you will accept where you are as your destination. And this is the worst tragedy in life. See your future before you start the journey of life. Myles Munroe said, "If what you see is no longer what you saw, then what you see is temporal." If what you are experiencing presently is no longer what you designed yesterday, then it is temporal. But how would you make this comparison, if you didn't design anything yesterday? Until you understand this truth, you may not succeed in life. Design your end. Though it sounds mechanical, yet a journey without an address will ever result in frustration. Write down your final address before you embark on this journey of success. Plan your future, see the accomplishment in your 'mind's eye', believe in yourself and write it down on paper. See it, say it, and read it until it is written in your mind. Then you are beginning to dream it, do it, be it, at this level you can throw the paper away and of a certainty you will fully become it. That is how to keep your faith alive!

ATTENTION: You will never learn this in the University or Polytechnic.

Friend, you can predict your future. You can create a way where there seems to be no way. You can invent tomorrow, if only you can carefully appropriate these mechanical yet result-oriented principles. Give this book to somebody you call a 'success' and he will unequivocally tell you that he appropriated the principles enlisted in it. Whatever you discover in this book is a key that has unlocked the destinies of those that are ahead of you. These are the reasons educated people live in poverty. They don't do the things that bring wealth. This book is a great 'Tool Box.' Use it!

Day 29 Exercise: Today, that dream that has been well written should be re-written boldly in an A3 paper. Read it, talk it, pray it, see it, believe it until you are becoming it in your mind and you will become it physically. After mapping out strategies for accomplishing your assignment, visualize its accomplishment in your mind. Do this until you are overwhelmingly aware of the joy of its accomplishment. Do it until something tells you that 'you are unstoppable.' And in reality nothing can stop you. Just try this, and you will be amazed at your results.

Day 30

Temperament: Use It! Don't Allow It To Use You.

I want to destroy a philosophy that has been accepted by many people. And this is the philosophy of temperament. Psychologist concluded that all men are grouped into four Temperaments and your temperament determines the type of job that you can do. According to them, the four groups are Sanguine, Choleric, Melancholic and Phlegmatic.

Let's summarize all in one paragraph: A Sanguine is very compassionate, talkative, warm, friendly, and carefree. They are also undisciplined, fearful, egotistical and unstable. They are only good in sales, acting and oratory. Choleric are very decisive, determined, confident, and optimistic. And they are also rude, proud, self-centered, self-sufficient and inconsiderate. They are only good in military, leadership, politics and architectural works. Melancholic are very talented, loyal, faithful, sensitive. They are also rigid, obstinate, critical, unsociable and negative. They are very creative, so Artists, Musicians, Inventors, Academicians and Philosophers fall into this group. Phlegmatic are humorous, efficient, quiet, committed to others yet unmotivated, passive, pessimistic and indecisive. Teachers, editors, doctors and accountants fall into this group.

All men are grouped into four Temperaments according to the Psychologists but this is not what will determine what you will become. Many educated people have stanched their destinies simply because they discovered they are doing jobs that are contrary to their temperaments. Uneducated people don't understand anything about this, so they believe that they can do any thing. It is not your temperament that determines your future. Anybody can sell a product or render a service. Temperaments can also be changed or modified. If temperament is a determinant factor for your destiny, then it can be changed or modified to suit your purpose on earth. Temperament is simply your inherent character, which can be worked on. Every character has its weakness and strength. How you control your weakness determines the fruit of your strength. So don't allow your temperament to stop you, rather, control or modify it.

The important thing is that you can succeed in life, irrespective of your temperament. It is not your understanding of your temperament that will make you what you want to be, but your understanding of the abilities in you. If your temperament is simply your inherent character, then I want you to note this: Character is formed from habit and habit is formed from subconscious actions. I repeat: Action is what you do. What you do subconsciously is what really forms your habit. And what you do subconsciously is directed from your subconscious mind. The same way what you do always can also affect your subconscious mind. What you do creates your habit, which later forms your character. To correct what you do, correct what you think. This in turn corrects what you do. Later it affects your habit and goes on to change your character. And once your character is changed your temperament has been modified. Reader, anyone can do anything! And any one can be wealthy. That is just it!

Day 30 Exercise: Today, start working on yourself. Those habits that are not congruent with what you want to become should be modified. Start acting as a wealthy person. Dress like one. Laugh like one. Watch your handshake. Start acting like a wealthy person. Greet like a millionaire. Hey, you've got to work on your temperament. Start from today.

Day 31
Stop Earning; Start Learning

There are two types of people on earth: learners and earners. Educated people are trained earners. The message in the school is: Be very serious so that you can graduate with a good grade and have a good job. What an erroneous message! You are either learning or earning. Earners are consumers; learners are investors. Earners usually work for money while learners make money work for them. Remember that you are either working for money or making your money to work for you. The difference is knowledge. In the world of success, knowledge is absolutely unavoidable. While I was reading Rich Dad Poor Dad, I saw the picture of my family and my life. The advice my parents have been giving to me is 'Make sure you get a good grade so that you can have a good job.' I knew that wasn't a good advice, but I was unable to convince them. As I grew up, I tried to share with people my view of life and success, but no one cared to listen. Every one seemed to give me the same advice my parents gave me. They viewed success as getting a good grade in the university. Some told me to go for professional exams. All I was told is to get more certificates. But most educated people I know are not successful. Even those that are viewed to be comfortable are so because they don't understand what success is all about. Remember one important point that I kept repeating in my first book. The point is this: If success were a product of education, then all professors would have become successful. People view success as being comfortable. Most of the people I met, usually associate success with having a good job in a reputable company, with an expensive car and a loving wife, in a good house and being able to send your children to the best schools on earth. I was really worried because I wasn't seeing life this way. I needed a confirmation from somebody, until I started reading Robert Kiyosaki's books.

As a young man looking for money to publish some of his books, I have been tempted to accept jobs that could give me more money. I have been tempted to work in places like the bank or an oil company where I could have most of the pleasures of life. Nobody wants to listen to me especially when I explained that I don't need job security. Most times I have been tempted to forget about my philosophy and accept whatever life offers. You will understand what I mean, if you are living in a country like Nigeria where you don't have control over many things. I have been given many names. But today, my philosophies are working. That is why I am sharing them with you.

Earners prefer security to control; learners prefer control to security. Earners seek for job security; learners seek for financial control. And in reality there is no job security, but there is financial control. The more secured we believe we are the less control we have over our finances and the less freedom we have. The Pension Reform Act 2004 that allows employee to save certain percentage of his or her salary for his or her retirement cannot and will never solve any problem. I wish they could use the money to buy knowledge for the employees. I wish they could teach them how to stop working for money and start making their money to work for them, to stop earning and start learning, and to stop increasing their liabilities and start increasing their assets, then the problem would be permanently solved. If you want to know more about why educated people make money mistakes and how you can overcome them, then order for my next book titled: Wealthy Barber Poor Professor.

It took 6,000 years to move from the Agricultural Age into Industrial Age, 150 years from the Industrial Age to Service age, 20 years from the Service Age to Information Age and 20 years later we entered the Information and Communication Age. Today, it's not your muscle power that produce result but your mind power. Not brute power but brainpower. That is why you can be active yet unproductive. It is not effort that counts but result. Physical power most times does not produce results. It is not the making and moving of things that brings result but the creation and dissemination of knowledge and ideas. The knowledge you have and your ability to communicate it will largely determine the quality of your life. According to Moore's Law in Computers, information processing capacity double every 18 months. And at the same time the cost of information processing drops by 50 percent. The consequence is that, if you rely on what you know you will soon faze out.

I want to repeat some of the things I have stated before, not because I do not have more things to write. I do have many things to explain about earning and learning. I have clearly, specifically and emphatically written on this topic in my book under the Missing Course series, titled, "If You Want to Be Wealthy, Don't Be a Graduate?" This book explains, contradicts and modifies most of our perceptions of life, money, knowledge and general success. I enjoin you to order for it because as I have stated before, this book you are reading is just a sequel to it. Here, I want to repeat some of the things I have stated before for more emphasis:

Learning is not schooling. Schooling is studying in a school. Learning is making life a school. Schooling gives you the certificate; learning gives you the skill. Schooling makes you educated; learning gets you informed. Many educated people are functional illiterates. Many educated people are either job seekers or job keepers. Some just work to earn a living. The problem with this nation is that we have too many educated people but very few are actually informed. You can survive with your education, you can rarely succeed with it, and you cannot be significant to this world until you are adequately informed.

Thomas Edison and Henry Ford were not educated. William Shakespeare was only a modern school graduate. Bill Gate was not a graduate before he became a success. I repeat: If greatness were a product of education, then all professors would have been great.

Information is the greatest asset. It is the link between where you are and where you want to be. Experience is never the best teacher. Don't be a victim before you learn. I repeat again, victors learn before a trend; victims learn after the trend. Understand that captains are controllers; captives are being controlled, the difference is knowledge. Remember that in the school of life there is no graduation. So keep learning, observing, and reading.

I want to summarize this segment below with the following life-changing paragraph. You may need to read it more than three times before you understand it very well. I borrowed some the philosophies from some millionaires. Just ponder on them!

You don't get in life what you want but you get what you are. You cannot do more than what you know. And what you know is what you are. Always learn to work harder on yourself than you do on your job. The harder you work on yourself, the smarter you work on your job. To have more than you've got, then become more than you are.

Day 31 Exercise: Today, you are going to make a vow to be using at least 5% of your earnings for learning. How? Begin by building your personal library. If you are finding it difficult in life, sell what you have left and use the money to buy books. If you don't know the books to buy, then send me an email. I will help you. If you are earning so well today, then prepare for the raining season. Not just by saving and investing alone, because you can loose both in one day. Start investing in your life. You will never loose it until you die. Your library is a treasure that will never fail.

Day 32
Start Placing God in The Right Place
About 1862, Count Ferdinand von Zeppelin, a German army officer, went to North America during the civil war. After his flight above the Mississippi River, he became fascinated, and changed his profession from military to building airships. During the innovation, many people mocked him but he persisted, and in July 1900 his first airship (Zeppelin) made its maiden flight. The government commended him, and even used his airship during the world war. The world was amazed at this great invention. A ship that is as tall as a 13-story building, with cabin for relaxation, 50-sitter dinning room, kitchen and others resources. 29 years later, Zeppelin flew around the world. As it is always said that in the world of commerce,

imitation has always been the highest form of flattery, before now, other countries joined in building airships. Britain manufactured R 101 and America manufactured Shenandoah, Akron and Macon. Airship was a success. But how reliable is the airship?

In 1925 U S lost her Shenandoah, and later lost Akron and Macon in 1933 and 1935 respectively. In 1930, Britain R 101 that took off to India crashed in France. It did not get to its destination. This shocked the entire World, but I wonder why it shocked the entire world. In 1937, the Hindenburg - Zeppelin's 37 years project - crashed, killing 36 passengers. The calamity just lasted for only 34 seconds.37 years of achievement was destroyed in 34 seconds and took 36 people to grave. What a tragedy! It baffles me whenever inventors assume that their inventions are reliable, and then put the entire world to dismay when they are proved to be wrong.

The story of Titanic that shocked the world in 1912 and put an end to British Wonder Ship should be a big lesson. The builder thought that it was 'unsinkable.' He was so sure of the world's biggest Ship that he questioned the need for lifeboats. He turned down every recommendation for safety measures. Though the Wonder Ship is a history today, but don't forget that it took more than 500 people to untimely grave. What is the lesson? Nothing can be reliable except God!

American - The police of the world. American - The giant of the entire earth. A country with the strongest security base. The most developed country. The citadel of technology. Yet September 11, 2001, would never be forgotten in the history of this great nation. You know what I mean. Terrorists attacked the World Trade Center in New York. Thousand of souls were destroyed. May their soul rest in peace. But what is the lesson? No one, anywhere, is truly safe. Safety is of the Lord!

Though it has been estimated that about 700 million people would be connected to the Internet in 2002, is the Internet Reliable? The answer is NO! In 1995, somebody stole information worth $1 million and 20,000 private Credit Card numbers. In Germany, T-online is one of the largest ISP with many customers across the world - including Nigeria, until a sixteen-year old boy with his friend penetrated into their database and got access to vital information. They announced to the world that T-online was wrong. Though T-online later built a more formidable security, however, it took only six hours before these two small boys broke the security again. Were these boys smarter than all the experts in T-online? No! What is the lesson?   Nothing   is   reliable,   except   God.

Friend, there is no source like God. He is "always available, ever reliable and eternally dependable." One thing I discovered in life is that experts always believe strongly in their expertise. They rely on proven theories. They act on the results of their experiments. Irrespective of your status, professionalism or intellectualism, always remember that there is none like God. What could be reliable in this world? Remember the fall of the Berlin Wall in 1989. Remember the Supersonic Concorde from Charles de Gaulle Airport in Paris, France that crashed into a hotel killing all on board and everyone in the hotel room on July 25, 2000. In Spain, on November 13, 2002, a sea oil Tanker - The Prestige - carrying 50,000 tons of oil broke and sank after it developed a leakage for six days. Remember that this has happened before: Aegean Sea sank near La Caruna in North Galacia, about ten years ago. And the Urquila sank with 100,000 tons of oil in 1976. What is the lesson? Wealth without God can vanish in a minute!

The only Source that will never fail is God. Your money will fail you, your personality will fail you, and man will fail you irrespective of the intimacy. Science and technology have failed and will continue to fail. You can be wealthy today and tomorrow morning you are the most wretched person on earth. Job in the Bible is a perfect example. He would explain this mystery best. Multinational companies have been drowned in the seas of life. I have seen great businessmen fall to the extent of begging for daily bread. It will never happen to you! Be practically involved in life; yet don't take the place of God. You have your part to play, but don't take the part of God. Don't take the place of God in your business and life. Don't ignore the finger of God in your life and business, so that He will not withdraw it from you. The greatest fallacy is the fallacy of self-made millionaire. You plant; God waters. Show it! It is called gratitude. If you refused to acknowledge God in your life, very soon nobody will remember you. I warn you!

Day 32 Exercise: Today, start developing the attitude of gratitude to God Almighty. There are problems that cannot be solved physically. This is a mystery that I cannot really explain. All I know is that only God will solve such problems. So you need Him. I have been faced with problems that I had to call God for help, Jesus Christ for courage and Holy Spirit for direction. This process is called fervent prayer. But it doesn't work until you have accepted Christ and made Him your best friend. I have read many books but I have not seen any book as resourceful as the Bible. Reader, you may need to do this particular exercise before that problem can be solved. Anyway, it's up to you!

Day 33
Study to Find Facts Not Fault
The greatest obstacle is to neglect all the obstacles or principles you have discovered in life. Avoid the obstacles but apply the principles. The ultimate key to success in life is to apply the keys you have already discovered. What differentiates millionaires from average people is that they always apply every proven success key. Most educated people always know what to do, but informed people do what they know. Application is the most productive key to any success. Learning is what converts efforts to results. And what differentiates learning from reading is application. Reader, we have come to the end of this part. However, don't neglect all that you have discovered. There are two ways to end a life on earth: One is 'Had I known.' The other is, 'I am glad I did.' The difference between the two is neglect. Life is systematic. The way to become great is to follow the footsteps of great people. Overcome these obstacles every true millionaires overcame, and soon you will become one. I enjoin you to accept these result-oriented principles I have outlined in this book. But I am sure that you will not neglect them. Coming this far with me, means that you are ready for a change. I know that many

educated people will read this book and find fault with almost everything in it. And that is the best reason they live in poverty. Informed people neglect faults and find facts; educated people neglect facts and find faults. You have a choice to make!

Let's conclude our journey, as we look at the 66 keys to success in life as deducted from this book. Your duty today is to read the conclusion of this book at least 3 times.

66 Keys to Success in Business and Life

1

Be practically involved in life, yet understand you have your part to play, but don't take the part of God. Don't take the place of God in your life.

2

Don't also ignore the finger of God in your life, so that He will not withdraw it from you. There are many routes to failure but the shortest of them all is to cheat others.

3

One of the secrets of successful people is that they don't learn too late

4

So don't wait to be a victim before you learn.

5

You cannot get something for nothing.

6

So never attribute success to luck or grace.

7

Don't wait for help. Don't wish for help. Don't look for help. Just work for help!

8
Be ready to make mistakes, and understand that no matter how painful a mistake is, there is always a gain behind it.

9
Don't pay more attention to caution else you will never advance in life.

10
In the road of success you will meet opposition, but never waste your time defending yourself.

11
If you wait to perfect everything before implementation, you may keep waiting till the end of the world.

12
You are going to fail many times, just understand that failure is an event not a person.

13
Always learn to use your today's pain for tomorrow's gain!

14
What is available to you is enough for a start, if you have enough ideas and confidence in yourself.

15
Every guru is a product of diligence. Be diligent, because diligence will always make a success out of a failure.

16
Success will always come your way, however, never sit down on the seat of success.

17

And never think like a successful person or you will soon fail.

18
Don't just work for money. Also make your money work for you.

19
Have control over your cash flow, and soon you will have financial freedom.

20
You must delay every immediate gratification for future benefits.

21
Your level of success is defined by your integrity not your dignity.

22
Integrity is knowing that everybody is important, and that no one is more important than another.

23
Success is a product of diversity. And diversity is doing one thing in different ways.

24
Have a website for your business. Very simple yet productive!

25
The future of every seed is in the soil. So also your future is highly dependable on the company you keep.

26
Always understand that any obstacle you predict in life is a question you must answer.

27
When things are difficult, don't change your project; change your strategies. Don't change the principles either; change the procedures. Change your techniques, your methods, your tactics. It counts!

28
There is nothing that is so important in the journey of success than to know that what you have is enough for the journey. Use it!

29
Turning your problems into projects is the major difference between success and failure. Do you have a problem? Make it a program.

30
Passion is what turns pressure into pleasure. So love what you do or do what you love.

31
Prepare before you start, because the quality of your preparation will always determine the degree of your manifestation.

32
Don't seek to be known, seek to know. When you know you will be known. You don't get in life what you want, but you get what you are. And what you know is what you are.

33
In life, you do not do your best and leave the rest. You have to do your plans and leave the rest.

34
. No one ever fails without a reason for his failure. But no reason is reasonable enough to fail.

35
All the things you need to advance in life will never be available. However, what is available is enough if you have confidence in yourself.

36
In life, indecision is not worst than wrong decision. Both will always lead to failure.

37

One productive decision, if implemented, may change the entire industry. So make that decision.

38
Get knowledge not education. Understand that the highest form of ignorance is to equate education with practicable business knowledge.

39
In the journey of success, a single innovation or advantage is never enough. If you want to have more than you've got, then become more than you are.

40
Every great man took great time to manifest his greatness. So be patient. For patience is the factory for greatness.

41
It is better to prepare for an opportunity and not have one, than to have an opportunity and not be prepared.

42
Shoot for the moon. Even if you miss it, you will land among the stars.

43
Always bear in mind that one of the greatest assets in life is not money but time.

44
Always remember that success is a collection of efforts and that there is no monopoly of ideas.

45
Personal development is the factory for skill, and skill is the producer of success. The harder you work on yourself, the smarter you will work on your job.

46

Practice is the fundamental principle for self-development. And stewardship is the place of practice. So always serve before you start.

47
Don't rob anybody; because you rob yourself the most, any time you rob others. To rob means to deny someone of what belongs or would belong to him or her, either by intimidation or manipulation.

48
No matter what you sell, people will buy because of the package but they will keep buying because of the value they derive from the product.

49
Every success is birthed by an idea.

50
And what differentiates an idea from ordinary thought is documentation.

51
Always set simple, specific, realistic, flexible and written goals.

52
As you determine your goal, from now upward your goal should determine what you do.

53
Distractions always come as opportunities. It takes commitment to differentiate between the two. So be committed!

54
Irrespective of your belief, you cannot undermine the part of mentorship in life.

55
One of the things that it takes to succeed in life is planning.

56

Planning in a simple term means thinking of how to use what you have to get what you want. Just think on paper!

57

Don't just plan your work; you must also work your plan. The therapy is called ACTION! So get up and get out!

58

Faith in God is the fundamental key to success in life. Yet success in life demands that you also have faith in yourself. Believe in yourself.

59

And having faith in yourself is determined by what you think. Remember, you are not what you think you are, you are what you think. To have faith in yourself, think positive about yourself.

60

It is not your temperament that determines your future. Anybody can sell a product or render a service. You too can!

61

Success in life demands that you stop earning and start learning. Because what you learn sustains what you earn.

62

No matter what you sell, try to add information products. It is not the making and moving of things that brings result but the creation and dissemination of knowledge and ideas. The knowledge you have and your ability to communicate it will largely determine your level of success in life.

63

Success is delivered to you most times on the platter of risk. And it is more risky not to take the risk

64

Don't undermine the power of asking. It is risk-free yet the starting engine for success in life. Don't beg but ask!

65

The ultimate key to success in life is to apply the keys you have already discovered. What differentiates wealthy people from average people is that they don't just know what to do, but they do what they know.

66

Educated people always neglect facts and find faults. Informed people neglect faults and find facts. I have given you 65 keys to success in life. But what do you see, faults or facts? You have a choice!

God bless you!
God bless Nigeria too!